Antonino Reggio (1725-ca1800)

Thematic Catalogue

-Edizione Antonino Reggio-

Anthony Hart

Antonino Reggio
(1725-ca1800)

Thematic Catalogue

-Edizione Antonino Reggio-
Valletta, 2013

www.monsignor-reggio.com

Copyright

Title :   Antonino Reggio (1725-ca1800) – Thematic Catalogue
Author: Anthony Hart
© 2013, Anthony Hart
Traduzione © 2013 Stefania Ferrara (it), Traduction © 2013 Dominique Hausfater (fr), Traducción © 2013 Jose Luis Fanju Rivero (es), Übersetzung© 2013 Prof. Dr. Cristina Urchueguía(ch)

Edizione Antonino Reggio
Mail: research@monsignor-reggio.com
Web: www.monsignor-reggio.com

ALL RIGHTS RESERVED. This book contains material protected under International and Federal Copyright Laws and Treaties. Any unauthorized reprint or use of this material is prohibited. No part of this book may be reproduced or transmitted in any form or by any means, electronic or mechanical, including photocopying, recording, or by any information storage and retrieval system without express written permission from the author / publisher

ISBN: 978-99957-0-515-2

 Table of Contents

Introduction (English)		3
Introduzione (italiano)		7
Einleitung (Deutsch)		11
Introduction (français)		15
Introducción (español)		19
I	Vocal Works	25
	1. Sacred Works by Genre/Title	27
	2. Secular Works by Title	29
	3. Vocal Works by Voices	31
II	Keyboard Sonatas	81
	1. Index by Key	83
III	Violoncello Sonatas	157
	1. Index by Key	159
IV	Lute Sonatas	173
	1. Index by Key	175

 Introduction:

This publication contains the thematic catalogue of the works of the eighteenth century Sicilian harpsichordist, violoncellist and composer Antonino Reggio. It is intended to be a companion to the biography, description of the works and further details of the sources; *'Eminent For His Skill in The Art, And Learning in The Science Of Sound: the life and music of Antonino Reggio'* (Edizione Antonino Reggio, Valletta, 2013).

It lists all of Reggio's known works with details of each one together with an incipit of the work in accordance with the conventions adopted by IAML (International Association of Music Libraries, Archives and Documentation Centres) and RISM (Répertoire International des Sources Musicales).

There are separate indexes for the different genres and the works are presented in order of the catalogue.

Catalogue and Numbering:

The works have been numbered with an Hr prefix and the numbering follows as close as possible the chronology of the date of composition, the majority of the early works being dated. The keyboard works are in the order of the volume numbers that Reggio designated, only one volume is dated. The lute and violoncello works are undated; these have been put as a separate category at the end of the series.

Antonino Reggio.

Antonino Reggio was born in Aci Catena, a commune in the province of Catania in Sicily, in 1725 and died, possibly in Rome in the last quarter of the 1700's, a member of a cadet branch of a Sicilian noble family, *Principi di Campofiorito*. He was a priest and in 1753 was assigned to the Apostolic Nuncio in Portugal. In 1763 Reggio relinquished his status of Abate with the monastery of Sant' Angelo di Brolo, and appointed to Monsignor.

Whilst in Rome he became well known as a composer and musician. In 1770 he was visited by the English musician and writer, Dr Charles Burney. Reggio is described as *'pretty good composer and performer on the harpsichord and violoncello'* and *'eminent for [his] skill in the art, and learning in the science of sound; among whom ...Monsignor Reggio.'* There appears to be little information regarding his ecclesiastical work in Rome. Reggio is also mentioned by the Roman poet and writer Giovanni Gherado De Rossi who describes Reggio as *' a man of great intellect, erudite, and very deep in music.'* The date of his demise is, as yet, unknown.

The majority of Reggio's 153 known original works are held in the Santini Collection in the Diözensanbibliothek, Münster.

Sources of Antonino Reggio's Works.

Diözesanbibliothek in Münster (RISM: D-MÜs).

The bulk of Reggio's works, eighteen manuscripts, containing some 150 works are to be found in the Santini- Collection of the Diözesanbibliothek in Münster. Thanks to the efforts of Klaus Kindler it has also been able to recognise Reggio's hand in the very important volumes of the keyboard sonatas of Domenico Scarlatti held in the collection.

Biblioteca Nazionale di Firenze (RISM: I-Fn).

A copy of the manuscript of *'Concertini a tre Soprani, e Contralto per le Signore Marchesine Laura, Prudenza, e Giacinta Astalli '* (Hr 27- Hr 46) is also held in the Biblioteca Nazionale di Firenze. The manuscript bears the title: *'Concerti a quattro Per Tre Soprani, e Contralto Di Monsignor Antonio Reggio'.* It is held under the reference of Mus 338. It was part of the private collection of Professor Giancarlo Rostirolla in Rome and was originally part of the collection of Ipolitto Galente.

Biblioteca da Palácio Nacional da Ajuda (RISM: P-La)

A second copy of the manuscript of 'Concertini' is held in the Biblioteca da Palácio Nacional da Ajuda, Lisbon. This manuscript is held under the reference: Manuscript 46-II-49.

This manuscript is an exact copy of the original in Münster and is also in Reggio's hand. It is unusual as it contains a printed title page and a dedication in Reggio's hand. The title on this page reads: *Concertini per Camera a Quattro Voci e Basso consagrati alla Maesta fedelissima di Giuseppe I Re di Portugallo e Algarvia'*

Monumento Nazionale di Montecassino (RISM: I-MC)

Four manuscripts, each containing three keyboard sonatas are held in the library of the Monastery of Montecassino. These works are copies of the sonatas contained in the first volume of Reggio's original works held in Münster (Hr 47-Hr 58). These are in a different hand to Reggio and also contain some slight variations in the score. The manuscriptS are held under the references: 6-F-8/6, 6-F-8/3, 6-F-8/2 and 6-A-1/15 The manuscripts were originally part of the collection of the abbot of the Monastery, Vincenzo Bovio. (1808 –1889),

Staatsbibliothek zu Berlin - Preußischer Kulturbesitz, Musikabteilung, Berlin (RISM: D-B)

A manuscript of ten movements are held by the Staatsbibliothek zu Berlin - Preußischer Kulturbesitz, Musikabteilung, Berlin under the reference of D-B/ Mus.ms.18165. These were original catalogued under the seventeenth century composer Pietro Reggio. He was born: 6 July 1632. died: 23 July 1685. The works have been identified as one complete sonata contained in the Santini- Collection of the Diözesanbibliothek in Münster and movements of other sonatas in the same collection.

Biblioteca Centrale della Regione Siciliana Palermo (RISM: I-PLn)

In the Biblioteca Centrale della Regione Siciliana Palermo there is a printed copy of a libretto for an azione sacra, Il Rè Mesa. Under the reference Misc. A. 234 132734 and entitled : *Il rè Mesa. Azione sacra da cantarsi nella chiesa del venerabile monastero di S. Niccolo l'Arena ... Musica del signor d. Antonino Reggio dei principi di Campofiorito.* No accompanying score has yet been found for this work.

 Introduzione

Con questa pubblicazione viene presentato il catalogo tematico delle opere del clavicembalista, violoncellista e compositore siciliano del diciottesimo secolo, Antonino Reggio. Esso è pensato essere una guida all'opera *Eminent For His Skill in The Art, And Learning in The Science Of Sound: the life and music of Antonino Reggio'* (Edizione Antonino Reggio, Valletta, 2013) che contiene la biografia, informazioni sulle sue opere e ulteriori dettagli sulle fonti documentali.

In questo catalogo sono elencati tutti i lavori conosciuti di Reggio con descrizioni e incipit secondo le convenzioni dettate dall'IAML (International Association of Music Libraries, Archives and Documentation Centres) e dal RISM (Répertoire International des Sources Musicales)

Ogni genere musicale possiede un proprio indice e le opere sono presentate in ordine di catalogo.

Catalogo e Numerazione

Le opere sono state numerate con un prefisso Hr seguendo il più possibile l'ordine cronologico delle date di composizione, essendo la maggior parte dei primi lavori provvisti di datazione. Le opere per strumenti a tastiera sono invece elencate secondo il numero di volume designato da Reggio stesso (solo un volume è datato). Le opere per liuto e violoncello non recano date e per questo sono state inserite in una categoria a parte alla fine del catalogo.

Antonino Reggio

Antonino Reggio nacque ad Aci Catena, un comune in provincia di Catania, in Sicilia, nel 1725 e morì probabilmente a Roma negli ultimi quindici anni del 1700. Era membro di un ramo cadetto della famiglia nobile siciliana i *Principi di Campofiorito*. Dopo aver preso i voti, nel 1753 fu affidato al Nunzio Apostolico in Portogallo. Nel 1763 Reggio rinunciò al suo status di abate presso il monastero di Sant'Angelo di Brolo e fu nominato Monsignor. Durante il soggiorno romano, divenne molto conosciuto come compositore e musicista.

Nel 1770 ricevette la visita dello scrittore e musicista inglese Charles Burney che descrisse Reggio con queste parole: "*un ottimo compositore e musicista di clavicembalo e violoncello*" – "*eminente per le [sue] abilità artistiche e per il sapere nella scienza del suono*". Tuttavia, sembrano esserci poche informazioni sul suo lavoro ecclesiastico a Roma. Reggio è stato inoltre citato dallo scrittore e poeta romano, Giovanni Gherado De Rossi che lo ha definito "*un uomo di sommo ingegno, di molta dottrina e profondo poi nella musica*".

La maggior parte dei lavori originali di Reggio fanno parte della collezione Santini, conservata presso la Diözensanbibliothek, a Münster.

Le fonti dei lavori di Antonino Reggio

Diözesanbibliothek a Münster (RISM: D-MÜs).
La maggior parte dei lavori di Reggio, diciottesimo manoscritti contenenti 152 partiture appartengono alla Collezione Santini della Diözesanbibliothek a Münster. Grazie agli studi di Klaus Kindler, è stata riconosciuta la firma di Reggio negli straordinari volumi delle sonate per tastiera di Domenico Scarlatti contenuti nella collezione.

Biblioteca Nazionale di Firenze (RISM: I-Fn).
Una copia del manoscritto di *Concertini a tre Soprani, e Contralto per le Signore Marchesine Laura, Prudenza, e Giacinta Astalli* '(Hr 27- Hr 46) è conservata anche nella Biblioteca Nazionale di Firenze. Il manoscritto reca il titolo *"Concerti a quattro Per Tre Soprani, e Contralto Di Monsignor Antonio Reggiò"* e il codice di riferimento è "Ms Mus 338". Questa trascrizione faceva parte della collezione privata del Professor Giancarlo Rostirolla di Roma ed apparteneva originariamente alla collezione di Ipolitto Galente.

Biblioteca da Palácio Nacional da Ajuda (RISM: P-La)
Una seconda copia del manoscritto di 'Concertini' è conservata nella Biblioteca da Palácio Nacional da Ajuda, Lisbona. Questo manoscritto reca il codice di catalogazione "Manoscritto 46-II-49". Si tratta di una copia esatta dell'originale di Münster trascritto personalmente da Reggio. È un lavoro insolito in quanto contiene il frontespizio stampato e una dedica autografata da Reggio. Il titolo recita: *"Concertini per Camera a Quattro Voci e Basso consagrati alla Maesta fedelissima di Giuseppe I Re di Portugallo e Algarviä"*.

Monumento Nazionale di Montecassino (RISM: I-MC)

Quattro manoscritti, ciascuno contenente tre suonate per tastiera, sono conservati nella biblioteca del monastero di Montecassino. Di questi, tre sono copie di sonate contenute nel primo volume dei lavori originali di Reggio conservati a Münster (Hr 47-Hr 58). Tuttavia essi sono stati trascritti da una mano diversa da quella di Reggio e contengono anche alcune sottili variazioni nello spartito. I manoscritti recano il codice di catalogo "6-F-8/6", "6-F-8/3", "6-F-8/2" e "6-A-1/15". Questi manoscritti originariamente facevano parte della collezione dell'abate del monastero, Vincenzo Bovio (1808–1889).

Staatsbibliothek zu Berlin - Preußischer Kulturbesitz, Musikabteilung, Berlin (RISM: D-B)

Un manoscritto contenente dieci movimenti è conservato presso la Staatsbibliothek zu Berlin - Preußischer Kulturbesitz, Musikabteilung, Berlin, con il codice "D-B/ Mus.ms.18165". Essi furono originariamente catalogati dal compositore del diciassettesimo secolo Pietro Reggio, (6 luglio 1632 - luglio 1685). I lavori sono stati identificati come una sonata completa della Collezione Santini del Diözesanbibliothek a Münster e come movimenti di altre sonate nella stessa collezione.

Biblioteca Centrale della Regione Sicilia a Palermo (RISM: I-PLn)

Nella Biblioteca Centrale della Regione Sicilia a Palermo è presente una copia stampata di un libretto dell'azione sacra, "Il Rè Mesa". Essa possiede il codice di catalogo "Misc. A. 234 132734" ed è intitolata: *Il rè Mesa. Azione sacra da cantarsi nella chiesa del venerabile monastero di S. Niccolo l'Arena ... Musica del signor d. Antonino Reggio dei principi di Campofiorito'.* Allo stato attuale elle ricerche non risultano spartiti di accompagnamento per quest'opera.

 **Einleitung**

Dieser Thematische Katalog verzeichnet die Werke des Antonino Reggio, einem sizilianischen Cembalist, Cellist und Komponist aus dem 18. Jh. Er ist als Beiheft zur Biographie: *'Eminent For His Skill in The Art, And Learning in The Science Of Sound: the life and music of Antonino Reggio'* (Edizione Antonino Reggio, Valletta, 2013) angelegt und trägt Werkbeschreibungen und weitere Quellenangaben bei. Es werden alle bekannten Werke detailliert und mit Angabe des Incipits aufgelistet nach den Vorgaben von IAML (International Association of Music Libraries, Archives and Documentation Centres) und RISM (Répertoire International des Sources Musicales).

Es stehen separate Indices nach Gattung und Werk zur Verfügung. Diese folgen der Ordnung des Kataloges.

Katalogzählung

Den Werke wurde jeweils ein Hr Präfix und eine Nummer zugeordnet, die so genau wie möglich der Chronologie der Enstehung folgt. Mehrheitlich sind die frühen Werke datiert. Die Tastenwerde werden gemäss der Reihenfolge in den Sammlungen geordnet, die Reggio selbst angelegt hat. Die Lauten und Cello Were sind nicht datiert, daher wurde sie in einer eigenen Abteilung verzeichnet am Ende der Serien.

Antonino Reggio.

Antonio Reggio wurde als Mitglied eines Nebenzweiges des sizilianischen Adelsgeschlechts *Principi di Campofiorito* in Aci Catena, einer Ortschaft der sizilianischen Provinz Catania 1725 geboren, er starb wahrscheinlich in Rom im letzten Viertel des 18. Jahrhundert. Er war Geistlicher, 1753 wurde er zum apostolischen Nuncius nach Portugal berufen. 1763 legte er das Amt des Laienabts des Klosters Sant'Angelo die Brolo nieder und nahm eine Ernennung als Monsignor an.

Während seines Romaufenthaltes wurde er als Komponist und Musiker sehr bekannt. 1770 statte ihm der englische Musiker und Musikpublizist Dr. Charles Burney einen Besuch. Reggio wird als 'ordentlicher Komponist und Interpret am Cembalo und Cello' beschreiben. Er zählt ihn unter den Leuten auf, 'die wegen ihrer Geschicklichkeit in der Ausübung, oder wegen ihrer Gelehrsamkeit in der Theorie der Musik hervorragen'. Seine Tätigkeit als Geistlicher in Rom scheint wenig dokumentiert zu sein. Reggio wurde auch von dem römischen Dichter und Schriftsteller Giovanni Gherardo De Rossi erwähnt, der ihn als „einen Mann grosser Erfindungsgabe, Kenntnis und tiefer Einsicht in die Musik'. Sein Todeszeitpunkt ist unbekannt.

Die Quellen von Antonino Reggios Werken

Diözesanbibliothek in Münster (RISM: D-MÜs).

Das grösste Corpus an Quellen zu Reggio, 18 Handschriften mit 150 Werken, befinden sich in der Santini-Sammlung der Diözesanbibliothek Münster. Es ist den Bemühungen von Klaus Kindler zu verdanken, dass die Handschrift von Reggio auch in den bedeutenden Bänden aus der Sammlung mit Cembalosonaten des Domenico Scarlatti identifiziert werden konnten.

Biblioteca Nazionale di Firenze (RISM: I-Fn).

Eine Kopie der Handschrift der *'Concertini a tre Soprani, e Contralto per le Signore Marchesine Laura, Prudenza, e Giacinta Astalli'* (Hr 27- Hr 46) befindet sich in der Biblioteca Nazionale di Firenze. Die Handschrift trägt dne Titel: *'Concerti a quattro Per Tre Soprani, e Contralto Di Monsignor Antonio Reggio'.* Sie wird unter der Signatur Mus 338 verwahrt. Sie gehörte zuvor der privaten Sammlung von Professor Giancarlo Rostirolla in Rom, und stammt ursprünglich aus der Sammlung des Ipolitto Galente.

Biblioteca da Palácio Nacional da Ajuda (RISM: P-La)

Eine zweite Abschrift der 'Concertini' wird in der Biblioteca da Palácio Nacional da Ajuda, Lissabon aufbewahrt. Die Handschrift trägt die Signatur: Manuscript 46-II-49.

Es handelt sich um eine getreue Kopie des Autographes aus Münster, die ebenfalls von Reggios Hand stammt. Sie ist insofern aussergewöhnlich, als sie ein gedrucktes Titelblatt und eine autographe Widmung Reggios enthält. Das Titelblatt lautet: *Concertini per Camera a Quattro Voci e Basso consagrati alla Maesta fedelissima di Giuseppe I Re di Portugallo e Algarvia'*

Monumento Nazionale di Montecassino (RISM: I-MC)
Vier Handschriften, die jeweils drei Cembalosonaten überliefern, befinden sich in der Bibliothek des Klosters Montecassino. Es handelt sich um Abschriften der Sonaten aus dem ersten Konvolut aus Münster (Hr 47-Hr 58). Es sind Kopistenhandschriften, die leichte Varianten aufweisen. Sie sind unter den Signaturen: 6-F-8/6, 6-F-8/3, 6-F-8/2 und 6-A-1/15 katalogisiert. Sie gehörten ursprünglich der Sammlung des Abts von Montecassino Vincenzo Bovio (1808 –1889).

Staatsbibliothek zu Berlin - Preußischer Kulturbesitz, Musikabteilung, Berlin (RISM: D-B)
Eine Handschrift mit zehn Einzelsätzen wird in der Staatsbibliothek zu Berlin - Preußischer Kulturbesitz, Musikabteilung, Berlin unter der Signatur of D-B/ Mus.ms.18165 verwahrt. Sie waren vormals dem Komponisten Pietro Reggio zugeschrieben, der im 17. Jh. nachgewiesen ist. Er legbte zwischen dem 6. Juli 1632 und dem 23. Juli 1685. Die Werke konnten als dank Konkordanzen in der Santini-Sammlung als Werke des Antonino Reggio identifiziert werden.

Biblioteca Centrale della Regione Siciliana Palermo (RISM: I-PLn)
Die Biblioteca Centrale della Regione Siciliana Palermo besitzt ein gedrucktes Exemplar des Libretto der *azione sacra, Il Rè Mesa* unter der Signatur: Misc. A. 234 132734. Der Titel lautet: *Il rè Mesa. Azione sacra da cantarsi nella chiesa del venerabile monastero di S. Niccolo l'Arena ... Musica del signor d. Antonino Reggio dei principi di Campofiorito'.* Es wurden bisher keine musikalischen Quellen nachgewiesen.

 **Introduction:**

Cette publication contient le catalogue thématique des œuvres du claveciniste, violoncelliste et compositeur sicilien du 18e siècle, Antonino Reggio. Elle est destinée à accompagner la biographie, le descriptif des œuvres et autres précisions sur les sources proposés dans : « *Eminent For His Skill in The Art, And Learning in The Science Of Sound: the life and music of Antonino Reggio'* (Edizione Antonino Reggio, Valletta, 2013).

Elle répertorie toutes les œuvres identifiées de Reggio, avec des précisions sur chacune et leur incipit, conforme aux conventions adoptées par l'AIBM (Association internationale des bibliothèques, archives et centres de documentation musicaux) et le RISM (Répertoire international des sources musicales).

Il y a des index pour chaque genre et les œuvres sont présentées dans l'ordre du catalogue.

Catalogue et numérotation

Le numéro des œuvres est précédé d'un préfixe Hr et la numérotation elle-même suit d'aussi près que possible la chronologie des dates de composition, la plupart des premières œuvres étant datées. Les pièces pour clavier suivent les numéros de volume indiqués par Reggio, seul l'un des volumes étant daté. Les pièces pour luth et pour violoncelle ne l'étant pas, elles font l'objet d'une section distincte à la fin de la série.

Antonino Reggio

Antonino Reggio, membre d'une branche cadette d'une noble famille sicilienne, les *Principi di Campofiorito*, est né en 1725 à Aci Catena, une commune de la province de Catane en Sicile, et est mort peut-être à Rome dans le dernier quart du 18e siècle. Il était prêtre et en 1753, fut nommé nonce apostolique au Portugal. Reggio abandonna son titre d'abbé du monastère de Sant'Angelo di Brolo en 1763 et fut nommé monsignor.

À Rome, il acquit une renommée comme compositeur et musicien. Il reçut en 1770 la visite du musicien et écrivain anglais Dr. Charles Burney qui le décrit comme un « *assez bon compositeur et interprète au clavecin et au violoncelle* » et précise : « *éminent par [son] talent dans l'art, et son érudition dans la science des sons ; dont fait partie... Monsignor Reggio* ». Il semble qu'il y ait peu d'informations concernant son activité ecclésiastique à Rome. Reggio est aussi mentionné par le poète et écrivain romain Giovanni Gherardo De Rossi, qui le décrit comme « *un homme d'une grande intelligence, érudit et très expérimenté en musique* ». La date de son décès demeure, pour le moment, inconnue.

Sources des œuvres d'Antonino Reggio

Diözensanbibliothek de Münster (RISM: D-MÜs).

La majeure partie des œuvres de Reggio, dix-huit manuscrits contenant quelque 150 pièces, se trouvent dans la Collection Santini de la Diözesanbibliothek de Münster. Grâce aux efforts de Klaus Kindler, il a également été possible d'identifier l'écriture de Reggio dans les très importants volumes des sonates pour clavier de Domenico Scarlatti conservés dans la collection.

Biblioteca Nazionale di Firenze (RISM: I-Fn).

Une copie du manuscrit des *Concertini a tre Soprani, e Contralto per le Signore Marchesine Laura, Prudenza, e Giacinta Astalli* (Hr 27- Hr 46) est également conservée à la Biblioteca Nazionale di Firenze. Le manuscrit porte le titre de *Concerti a quattro Per Tre Soprani, e Contralto Di Monsignor Antonio Reggio* et la cote Mus 338. Il faisait partie de la collection particulière du professeur Giancarlo Rostirolla à Rome et, à l'origine, de celle d'Ipolitto Galente.

Biblioteca da Palácio Nacional da Ajuda (RISM: P-La)

Une seconde copie du manuscrit des *Concertini* est conservée à la Biblioteca da Palácio Nacional da Ajuda, Lisbonne sous la cote : Manuscript 46-II-49. Ce manuscrit est une copie fidèle de l'original à Münster et également de la main de Reggio. Bizarrement, il porte une page de titre imprimée et une dédicace autographe du compositeur. Le titre exact est : *Concertini per Camera a Quattro Voci e Basso consagrati alla Maesta fedelissima di Giuseppe I Re di Portugallo e Algarvia*.

Monumento Nazionale di Montecassino (RISM: I-MC)
Quatre manuscrits contenant chacun trois sonates pour clavier sont conservés à la bibliothèque de l'abbaye du Mont-Cassin. Ces oeuvres sont des copies de celles figurant dans le premier volume des oeuvres originales de Reggio conservées à Münster (Hr 47-Hr 58). Elles sont d'une autre main et présentent également quelques variantes mineures dans la partition. Les manuscrits sont conservés sous les cotes 6-F-8/6, 6-F-8/3, 6-F-8/2 and 6-A-1/15 et faisaient, à l'origine, partie de la collection de l'abbé du monastère, Vincenzo Bovio (1808-1889).

Staatsbibliothek zu Berlin - Preußischer Kulturbesitz, Musikabteilung, Berlin (RISM: D-B)
Un manuscrit contenant dix mouvements est conservé à la Staatsbibliothek zu Berlin - Preußischer Kulturbesitz, Musikabteilung, Berlin, sous la cote D-B/ Mus.ms.18165. Ils avaient initialement été catalogués sous le nom du compositeur du 17e siècle Pietro Reggio, né le 6 juillet 1632 et mort le 23 juillet 1685. Les pièces ont pu être identifiées comme une sonate complète de la collection Santini de la Diözesanbibliothek de Münster et des mouvements séparés d'autres sonates de la même collection.

Biblioteca Centrale della Regione Siciliana Palermo (RISM: I-PLn)
Il existe, à la Biblioteca Centrale della Regione Siciliana de Palerme, un exemplaire imprimé du livret d'un oratorio, *Il Rè Mesa*, conservé sous la cote Misc. A. 234   132734 et s'intitulant : *Il rè Mesa. Azione sacra da cantarsi nella chiesa del venerabile monastero di S. Niccolo l'Arena ... Musica del signor d. Antonino Reggio dei principi di Campofiorito*. Aucune partition n'en a été retrouvée pour le moment.

 **Introducción:**

Esta publicación contiene el catálogo temático de las obras del clavecinista, violoncelista y compositor siciliano del siglo dieciocho Antonino Reggio. Dirigido para ser un complemento de la biografía, donde se incluye la descripción de las obras y otros detalles de las fuentes; *"Eminente por sus habilidades en el arte, y maestro en la ciencia del sonido: la vida y música de Antonino Reggio"* (Edición Antonino Reggio, Valleta, 2013).

El catálogo relaciona las obras más conocidas de Reggio con detalles de cada una, junto con un incipiente trabajo que prosigue a las convenciones de la IAML (Asociación Internacional de Bibliotecas de Música, Archivos y Centros de Documentación) y RISM (Repertorio Internacional de Fuentes Musicales).

Existen índices separados para cada uno de los géneros y las obras son presentadas en un orden de catalogación.

Catálogo y Numeración:

Las obras han sido numeradas con un código Hr y la numeración sigue tan cercana posible la cronología de la fecha de composición, la mayoría de las obras tempranas han sido fechadas. Las obras para teclado aparecen en orden de volumen que Reggio designó, sólo un volumen es fechado. Las partituras para laúd y violonchelo no son fechadas; y han sido puestas como una categoría separada en el final de las series.

Antonino Reggio.

Antonio Reggio nació en Aci Catena, una comuna de la provincia de Catania en Sicilia, en 1725 y murió, posiblemente en Roma en el último cuarto del siglo dieciocho, un miembro del cuerpo de cadetes de una aristocrática familia siciliana, *Principi di Campofiorito*. Fue un sacerdote, y en 1753 fue asignado al Nuncio Apostólico en Portugal. En 1763 Reggio renunció a su estatus de abad con el monasterio de Sant´ Angelo di Brolo, y fue propuesto a Monseñor.

Mientras vivió en Roma, se convirtió en un reconocido músico y compositor. En 1770 fue visitado por el músico y escritor inglés Dr. Charles Burney. Reggio es descrito como *"muy buen compositor e intérprete en el clavicémbalo y violoncello"* y *"eminente por (sus) habilidades en el arte y enseñanza en la ciencia del sonido: de todos... Monseñor Reggio"*. Esta precisa información refiere a su obra eclesiástica in Roma. Reggio es también mencionado por el poeta y escritor romano Giovanni Gherardo De Rossi, quien lo describe como *"un hombre de gran intelecto, erudito, y muy profundo en la música"*. La fecha de su fallecimiento es, aún, desconocida.

La mayoría de las 153 obras originales conocidas de Reggio son conservadas en la Colección Santini en en Münster.

Obras manuscritas de Antonino Reggio.

Diözesanbibliothek in Münster (RISM: D-MÜs).

La mayor parte de las obras de Reggio, dieciocho manuscritos, contienen algunas 150 partituras que pueden ser encontradas en la Colección Santini de la Biblioteca Diocesana en Münster. Gracias a los esfuerzos de Klaus Kindler también están disponibles para reconocer las manos de Reggio en el importante volumen de las sonatas para teclado de Doménico Scarlatti preservadas en la colección.

Biblioteca Nacional de Florencia (RISM: I-Fn).

Una copia del manuscrito de *"Concertino a tres sopranos y contralto para la Señora Marchesine Laura, Prudenza, e Giacinta Astalli"* (Hr 27- Hr 46) es también conservado en la Biblioteca Nacional de Florencia. El manuscrito contiene el título: *'Concerti a quattro Per Tre Soprani, e Contralto Di Monsignor Antonio Reggio'.* Está registrado con la referencia de Mus 338.

Biblioteca del Palacio Nacional de Ajuda (RISM: P-La)

Una segunda copia del manuscrito de "Concertino" es conservada en la Biblioteca del Palacio Nacional de Ajuda, Lisboa. Este documento está registrado bajo la referencia: Manuscrito 46-II-49.

Este ejemplar es una copia exacta del original en Münster y es también escrito a mano de Reggio. Esto es inusual como contiene un título impreso en la página y la dedicación por sus manos. El título en estas páginas dice: *"Concertini per Camera a Quattro Voci e Basso consagrati alla Maesta fedelissima dei Giuseppe I Re di Potugallo e Algarvia".*

Monumento Nacional de Montecassino (RISM: I-MC)
Cuatro manuscritos, cada uno contiene tres sonatas para teclado, y son atesorados en la librería del Monasterio de Montecassino. Estas obras son copias de las sonatas incluidas en el primer volumen de las obras originales de Reggio archivadas en Münster (Hr). Estas están copiadas no por Reggio y también contienen algunas ligeras variaciones en la partitura. El manuscrito es conservado bajo la referencia: 6-F-8/6, 6-F-8/3, 6-F-8/2 y 6-A-1/15. Los manuscritos fueron originalmente parte de la colección del abad del Monasterio, Vicenzo Bovio. (1808-1889).

Staatsbibliothek zu Berlin - Preußischer Kulturbesitz, Musikabteilung, Berlin (RISM: D-B)
Un manuscrito de diez movimientos se conserva en la Staatsbibliothek zu Berlin - Preußischer Kulturbesitz, Musikabteilung, Berlin, bajo la referencia de D-B/ Mus.ms.18165. Estos fueron originalmente catalogados por el compositor del siglo diecisiete Pietro Reggio. Este músico nació el 6 de julio de 1632, y murió el 23 de julio de 1685. Las obras han sido identificadas como una sonata completa incluida en la Colección Santini de la Biblioteca Diocesana en Münster y los movimientos de otras sonatas aparecen en la misma colección.

Biblioteca Centrale della Regione Siciliana Palermo (RISM: I-PLn)
En la Biblioteca Centrale della Regione Siciliana Palermo existe una copia impresa de un libreto para una *azione sacra*, Il Rè Mesa. Bajo la referencia Misc. A. 234 132734 y titulada: *Il rè Mesa. Azione sacra ... venerabile monastero di S. Niccolo l'Arena ... Musica del signor d. Antonino Reggio dei principi di Campofiorito*. No se ha encontrado una partitura que acompañe para esta obra.

I

Vocal Works

II

Keyboard Sonatas

III

Violoncello Sonatas

IV

Lute Sonatas

I Vocal Works

1. Sacred Works

    By Genre/Title

2. Secular Works

    By Title

3. Vocal Works by Voice

    By Voices

1.Sacred Works: Index by Genre/Title

Sacred Cantata:
    E fin a quando o Dio   Hr 2

Psalms:
    Dixit Dominus   Hr 15
    Domine ad Adjuvandum   Hr 14

Motet:
    Iube Domne benedicere   Hr 26

Masses:
    Mass in G major   Hr 7 Hr 16

Antiphon;
    Salve Regina   Hr 5

Intermezzi Sacri:
    Il Sacrifizio di Gefte   Hr 13
    La Decollazione di S Giovanni Battista   Hr 18
    Giuseppe riconosciuto   Hr 19
    Il Re Mesa   Hr Misc 1

2. Secular Works Index by Title

Ah se di te mi privi	Hr 34 Hr 45
Ah che vuol dir quel pianto	Hr 38
Amo te solo	Hr 12
Cara non tanto sdegno	Hr 42
Che non mi disse un dì	Hr 6
Crudel morir mi vedi	Hr 35
Crudo amor oh dio ti sento	Hr 3
Digli ch'io son fedele	Hr 11
Io scordarmi il mio diletto	Hr 46
La destra ti chiedo	Hr 30
La Gelosia	Hr 21
L'estremo pegno almeno	Hr 43
Mio ben ricordati	Hr 24
Mille volte o mio tesoro	Hr 32
Misero me qual vero aspetto	Hr 25
Ne' giorni tuoi felici	Hr 29
Non temer ch'io mai ti dica	Hr 10
Non temer non son più amante	Hr 27
Per conforto a tanti quai	Hr 9
Perché se re tu sei	Hr 41
Sappi ch'al nascer mio	Hr 40
Scocca o cielo ardenti strali	Hr 44
Se a te penso o paradiso	Hr 17
Se del fiume altera l'onda	Hr 23
Se mai turbo il tuo riposo	Hr 36
Se tutti i miei pensieri	Hr 4
Sì ti credo amato bene	Hr 31
Sì ti fido al tuo gran core	Hr 39
Tu vuoi ch'io viva o cara	Hr 28
Va ti consola addio	Hr 33
Vanne a regnar ben mio	Hr 37
Voglio al tuo fianco ogn'ora vivere	Hr 8

2. Vocal Works Index by Voice

Solo:

    Alto: Hr 2 Hr 24

    Soprano: Hr 3 Hr 4 Hr 5 Hr 6 Hr 8
                                 Hr 9 Hr 10 Hr 11 Hr 12
                                 Hr 17 Hr 21 Hr 23 Hr 26

Duets:

    Soprano (2):   Hr 20 Hr 25

Trio:

    Soprano (3):   Hr 13 Hr 18 Hr 19

    Soprano (2) / Alto: Hr 22

Quartets:

    Soprano (3) / Alto: Hr 27 – Hr 46

    Soprano, Alto,
    Tenor, Bass: Hr 7 Hr 14 Hr 15 Hr 16

Quartets with Choir:

    Soprano (3) / Alto :   Hr 1

    Soprano, Alto,
    Tenor, Bass: Hr 7 Hr 14 Hr 15 Hr 16

Lodi al gran Dio d'Abramo

Catalogue No:	Hr 1
Date:	1745
Key:	G Major
Scoring:	Soprano (3), Alto, Coro Soprano (3), Coro Alto, violin 1, violin 2, viola, bass flute (2), oboe (2), horn(2)
Text:	Drago, Casimiro
Language:	Italian
Genre:	Cantatas
Source description:	
Original title:	*Dialogo a 4 Voci / con VV ed altri Stromenti / del Sigr N: N: / [at bottom right:] Poesia del Sigr Marchese D. Casimiro Drago / [at head left:] Reggio / [at head right:] Anno 1745.*
Material:	Manuscript, Autograph, score: 67f.

Incipits

1.1.1 Violin, c Introduzione; G major

1.2.1 Soprano coro, 3/8 G major

Lodi al gran Dio d'Abramo

Roles:	Menacla (Soprano), Elpino (Soprano), Angelo (Soprano), Montano (Alto), Coro d'Angeli
Library:	Santini-Sammlung, Diözesanbibliothek, Münster
Siglum/ signature:	D-MÜs/ SANT Hs 3384

E fin a quando o Dio

Catalogue No:	Hr 2
Date:	1745
Key:	F Major
Scoring:	Alto, violin 1, violin 2, viola, basso continuo
Language:	Italian
Genre:	Sacred Cantatas

Source description:

Original title: *[caption title:] di Reggio / Cantata Sacra a Voce / di Contralto con V:V: 1745 in Palermo.*

Material: Manuscript, Autograph, score: 8f.

Incipits

1.1.1 Alto, c [Recitative];

E fin a quando o Dio

1.2.1 violin 1, c/ [Aria]. Un poco lento; F major

1.2.2 Alto, c/ F major

Mentre penso al vostro regno

Library: Santini-Sammlung, Diözesanbibliothek, Münster

Siglum/ signature: D-MÜs/ SANT Hs 3382 (Nr. 10)

Notes:
Annotated: "per la Sigra N. N."

Crudo amor oh Dio ti sento

Catalogue No:	Hr 3
Date:	1746
Key:	C minor
Scoring:	Soprano, violin 1, violin 2, viola, bass
Text:	Metastasio, Pietro
Language:	Italian
Genre:	Arias

Source description:

Original title: *[heading:] Palermo 1746 / Del Sig^r N. N. [later changed in:] D. Ant^o Reggio.*

Material: Manuscript, Autograph, score: 4f.

Incipits:

1.1.1 violin, 3/4 [Aria]. Andante amoroso; C minor

1.1.2 Soprano, 3/4 C minor

Crudo amor oh dio ti sento

Library:	Santini-Sammlung, Diözesanbibliothek, Münster
Siglum/ signature:	D-MÜs/ SANT Hs 3382 (Nr. 2)

Notes:

The text is from Pietro Metastasio's "Issipile" Scene XIV, Act 1

Se tutti i miei pensieri

Catalogue No:	Hr 4
Date:	1746
Key:	A major
Scoring:	Soprano, violin 1, violin 2, viola, bass
Text:	Metastasio, Pietro
Language:	Italian
Genre:	Arias

Source description:

Original title: [heading:] Palermo 1746

Material: Autograph: 1746 (1746), score: 4f.

Incipits:

1.1.1 violin 1, c. [Aria]. Cantabile; A major

1.1.2 Soprano, c A major

Se tutti i miei pensieri

Library: Santini-Sammlung, Diözesanbibliothek, Münster

Siglum/ signature: D-MÜs/ SANT Hs 3382 (Nr. 3)

Notes:

The text is from Pietro Metastasio's "Demetrio" Scene X, Act 3

Salve Regina

Catalogue No:	Hr 5
Date:	1747
Key:	E♭ major
Scoring Note:	Soprano, violin (2), viola, bass
Language:	Latin
Genre:	Antiphons
Source description:	
Original title:	*Salve Regina / a Voce sola di Soprano / con VV: Sigr D: Antonino Reggio / 20 Aprile 1747.*
Material:	Manuscript, Autograph, score: 11f.

Incipits:

1.1.1 violin 1, 3/4 Moderato; E♭ major

1.1.2 S, 3/4 Moderato; E♭ major

Salve regina, mater misericordiae vita dulcedo

Library:	Santini-Sammlung, Diözesanbibliothek, Münster
Siglum/ signature:	D-MÜs/ SANT Hs 3514 (Nr. 1)

Notes:
Annotated: "20 Maggio 1747", "Composta per S. C. Principessa di Campofiorito"
Dedicatee: Caterina Gravina, , Principessa di Campofiorito

Che non mi disse un dì

Catalogue No:	Hr 6
Date:	1747
Key:	C minor
Scoring:	Soprano, violin 1, violin 2, viola, bass
Text:	Metastasio, Pietro
Language:	Italian
Genre:	Arias

Source description:

Original title:	*[heading:] in Palermo 1747 per la Sig^{ra} N. N. [right:] Reggio.*
Material:	Manuscript, Autograph, score: 6f.

Incipits:

1.1.1 violin 1, c [Aria]. Allegretto; C minor

1.1.2 Soprano, c C minor

Che non mi disse un dì

Library:	Santini-Sammlung, Diözesanbibliothek, Münster
Siglum/ signature:	D-MÜs/ SANT Hs 3382 (Nr. 8)

Notes:
The text is from Pietro Metastasio's "Olimpiade" Scene IV, Act 2

Mass in G major

Catalogue No:	Hr 7
Date:	1748
Key:	G major
Scoring Note:	Soprano, Alto, Tenor, Bass, Choir: Soprano, Alto, Tenor, Bass, violin 1, violin 2, viola, horn (2), basso continuo: organ
Language:	Latin
Genre:	Masses
Source description:	
Original title:	*Messa a 4 Voci con V: V: / Violetta, Basso e Corni / Del Sig:r N. N: / Aci Catena 26 Agosto 1748.*
Material:	Manuscript, Autograph, score: 39f.

Incipits:

1.1.1 violin 1, c Allegretto; G major

1.1.2 Soprano, c G major

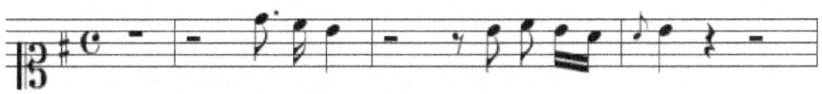

Kyrie, eleison Christe eleison Kyrie eleison

Library:	Santini-Sammlung, Diözesanbibliothek, Münster
Siglum/ signature:	D-MÜs/ SANT Hs 3378

Notes:
Annotated top left: "Originale"

Voglio al tuo fianco ogn'ora vivere

Catalogue No:	Hr 8
Date:	1748
Key:	D major
Scoring:	Soprano, violin 1, violin 2, viola, bass
Language:	Italian
Genre:	Arias

Source description:

Original title: [heading:] *Palermo 1748 / Reggio.*

Material: Manuscript, Autograph, score: 4f.

Incipits:

1.1.1 violin, 3/8 [Aria]. Allegro affettuoso; D major

1.1.2 Soprano, 3/8 D major

Voglio al tuo fianco ogn'ora vivere

Library: Santini-Sammlung, Diözesanbibliothek, Münster

Siglum/ signature: D-MÜs/ SANT Hs 3382 (Nr. 4)

Notes:
Annotated: "Per la Sig[ra] Principessina di Poggioreale"
Dedicatee: Principessina di Poggioreale

Per conforto a tanti quai

Catalogue No:	Hr 9
Date:	1748
Key:	E major
Scoring:	Soprano, violin 1, violin 2, viola, bass
Language:	Italian
Genre:	Arias
Source description:	
Original title:	*[heading:] in Palermo 1748 per la Sig^{ra} Duchessa Geli.*
Material:	Manuscript, Autograph, score: 4f.

Incipits:

1.1.1 violin 1, 3/8 [Aria]. Allegretto; E major

1.1.2 Soprano, 3/8 E major

Per conforto a tanti quai

Library:	Santini-Sammlung, Diözesanbibliothek, Münster
Siglum/ signature:	D-MÜs/ SANT Hs 3382 (Nr. 5)

Notes:
Dedicatee: Duchessa Geli, (possibly Gela)

Non temer ch'io mai ti dica

Catalogue No:	Hr 10
Date:	1748
Key:	E♭ major
Scoring:	Soprano, violin 1, violin 2, viola, bass
Text:	Metastasio, Pietro
Language:	Italian
Genre:	Arias

Source description:

Original title:	*[heading:] in Palermo 1748 per la Sig^ra N. N. [right:] Reggio.*
Material:	Manuscript, Autograph, score: 4f.

Incipits:

1.1.1 violin 1, 3/8 [Aria]. Allegretto; E♭major

1.1.2 Soprano, 3/8 E♭ major

Non temer ch'io mai ti dica

Library:	Santini-Sammlung, Diözesanbibliothek, Münster
Siglum/ signature:	D-MÜs/ SANT Hs 3382 (Nr. 6)

Notes:
The text is from Pietro Metastasio's "Artaserse" Scene V act 2

Digli ch'io son fedele

Catalogue No:	Hr 11
Date:	1748
Key:	F major
Scoring:	Soprano, violin 1, violin 2, viola, bass
Text:	Metastasio, Pietro
Language:	Italian
Genre:	Arias

Source description:

Original title:	*[heading:] in Palermo 1748 per la Sig^ra Duchessa Geli [right:] Reggio.*
Material:	Manuscript, Autograph, score: 4f.

Incipits:

1.1.1 violin 1, c [Aria]. Andante grazioso; F major

1.1.2 Soprano, c F major

Digli ch'io son fedele

Library:	Santini-Sammlung, Diözesanbibliothek, Münster
Siglum/ signature:	D-MÜs/ SANT Hs 3382 (Nr. 7)

Notes:
The text is from Pietro Metastasio's "Alessandro nell'Indie" Scene IX, Act 2
Dedicatee: Geli, Duchessa (possibly Gela)

Amo te solo

Catalogue No:	Hr 12
Date:	1748
Key:	F major
Scoring:	Soprano, violin 1, violin 2, viola, bass
Text:	Metastasio, Pietro
Language:	Italian
Genre:	Arias

Source description:

Original title:	*[heading:] Palermo 1748 per la Sig^{ra} N. N. / Reggio.*
Material:	Manuscript, Autograph, score: 5f.

Incipits:

1.1.1 violin 1, 2/4 [Aria]. Andante grazioso; F major

1.1.2 Soprano, 2/4 F major

Amo te solo

Library:	Santini-Sammlung, Diözesanbibliothek, Münster
Siglum/ signature:	D-MÜs/ SANT Hs 3382 (Nr. 9)

Notes:
The text is from Pietro Metastasio's "La Clemenza di Tito" Scene VII, Act 1

Il Sacrifizio di Gefte

Catalogue No:	Hr 13
Date:	1749
Key:	C Major
Scoring:	Soprano(3), violin 1, violin 2, viola, horn (2), bc
Language:	Italian
Genre:	Azione Sacra

Source description

Original title:	Il Sacrifizio di Gefte | Intermezzo Sacro | a 3 Voci con V: V: Violetta, Basso | e Corni da Caccia di D. Anto Reggio.
Material:	Manuscript, Autograph, score: 31f.

Incipits

1.1.1 S, c Gefte; Rec..;

Con strepitosi suoni non più assordino

1.2.1 S, 3/4 Figlia di Gefte; Aria.;

Se canti e suoni s'intoni invita

Library:	Santini-Sammlung, Diözesanbibliothek, Münster
Siglum/ signature:	D-MÜs/ SANT Hs 3379 (Nr. 1)

Notes:
Roles: Telandro (S)
Annotated top left: "1749" and top right: "*Originale*"

Domine ad Adjuvandum

Catalogue No:	Hr 14
Date:	1749
Key:	G major
Scoring:	Soprano, Alto, Tenor, Bass, violin 1, violin 2, viola, horn (2), organ, basso continuo: organ
Language:	Latin
Genre:	Psalms

Source description:

Original title: *Domine ad adjuvandum etc. / a 4 Voci con Violini / Violetta, Organo e / Corni da Caccia / Del Sig:r N: N: Anno 1749 16 Gennaro.*

Material: Manuscript, Autograph, score: 10f.

Incipits:

1.1.1 S, c/ Allegro non presto; G major

Domine ad adjuvandum, me festina

Library: Santini-Sammlung, Diözesanbibliothek, Münster

Siglum/ signature: D-MÜs/ SANT Hs 3380 (Nr. 1)

Notes:
Annotated top right: "Originale.

Dixit Dominus

Catalogue No:	Hr 15
Date:	1749
Key:	D major
Scoring Note:	Soprano, Alto, Tenor, Bass, violin 1, violin 2, viola, trumpet (2), basso continuo: organ
Language:	Latin
Genre:	Psalms
Source description:	
Original title:	*Dixit a 4 Voci con V: V: / Violetta, Organo e Trombe / del Sig:r N: N: / Alli 9 Gennaro 1749.*
Material:	Manuscript, Autograph, score: 33f.

Incipits:

1.1.1 violin 1, c Allegro; D major

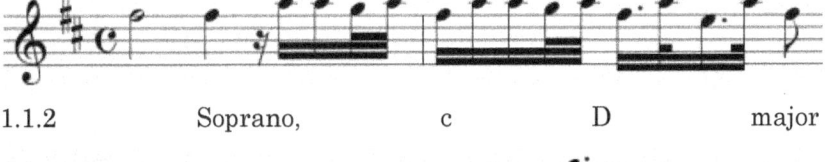

1.1.2　　　　Soprano,　　　　c　　　　D　　　　major

Dixit Dominus, Domino meo sede a dextris meis

Library:	Santini-Sammlung, Diözesanbibliothek, Münster
Siglum/ signature:	D-MÜs/ SANT Hs 3380 (Nr. 2)

Further notes:
Annotated top right: "Originale"

Mass in G major

Catalogue No:	Hr 16
Date:	1750
Key:	G major
Scoring Note:	Soprano, Alto, Tenor, Bass, Choir : Soprano, Alto, Tenor, Bass, violin 1, violin 2, viola, horn (2), basso continuo: organ
Language:	Latin
Genre:	Masses
Source description:	
Original title:	*Messa a 4 Voci con V: V: / Violetta Corni da Caccia / ed Organo [added by Santini:] Antonio Reggio.*
Material:	Manuscript, Autograph, score: 37f.

Incipits:

1.1.1 violin 1, c/ Andante; G major

1.1.2 Soprano, c/ G major

Kyrie, eleison Christe eleison Kyrie eleison

Library:	Santini-Sammlung, Diözesanbibliothek, Münster
Siglum/ signature:	(D-MÜs/ SANT Hs 3377)

Notes:
Annotated top left: "Originale"; top right: "Nell' Aprile del 1750"

Se a te penso o paradiso

Catalogue No:	Hr 17
Date:	1750
Key:	B♭ major
Scoring:	Soprano, violin 1, violin 2, viola, basso continuo
Language:	Italian
Genre:	Arias

Source description:

Original title:	*[heading:] 1750. Reggio [right:] Originale.*
Material:	Manuscript, Autograph, score: 4f.

Incipits:

1.1.1 violin 1, 3/4 [Aria]. Lento; B♭ major

1.1.2 Soprano, 3/4 B♭ major

Se a te penso o paradiso

Library:	Santini-Sammlung, Diözesanbibliothek, Münster
Siglum/ signature:	D-MÜs/ SANT Hs 3382 (Nr. 1)

La Decollazione di S Giovanni Battista

Catalogue No:	Hr 18
Date:	[n.d]
Key:	C Major
Scoring:	Soprano (3), violin 1, violin 2, viola, bc
Language:	Italian

Source description

Original title:	La Decollazione di S: Gio: Battista | Intermezzo Sacro a 3 Voci | con V: V: Violetta, Basso | e Corni da Caccia.
Material:	Manuscript, Autograph, score: 28f.

Incipits

1.1.1 S, c Erode; Recitive..;

Erodiade bella

1.2.1 S, c Erode; Aria. Andante;

Quel che vorrai sì tutto avrai

Library:	Santini-Sammlung, Diözesanbibliothek, Münster
Siglum/ signature:	D-MÜs/ SANT Hs 3379 (Nr. 3)

Notes:
Roles: Erodiade (S), Erodiade Figlia (S)
 Annotated top right: "*Originale*". Mentioned on the title page but the *Corni da Caccia* not shown in the score.

Giuseppe riconosciuto

Catalogue No:	Hr 19
Date:	1751
Key:	C Major
Scoring:	Soprano(3), violin 1, violin 2, viola, horn(2), bc
Language:	Italian

Source description

Original title:	*Giuseppe Riconosciuto / Intermezzo a tre Personaggi.*
Material:	Manuscript, Autograph, score: 23f.

Incipits

1.1.1 S, c Giuseppe; Rec..;

Tu che dell'alme nostre eterna verità

1.2.1 vl 1, c/ Aria. Andante;

1.2.2 S, c/

Sarò qual madre amante

Library:	Santini-Sammlung, Diözesanbibliothek, Münster
Siglum/ signature:	D-MÜs/ SANT Hs 3379 (Nr. 2)

Notes:
Annotated top: "*Originale di D. Antonio Reggio*" and right: "1751"

Tantum ergo

Catalogue No:	Hr 20
Date:	[n.d.]
Key:	G major
Scoring:	Soprano (2), organ
Language:	Latin
Genre:	Hymns
Source description:	
Original title:	*Tantum ergo / a due Soprani / ed / Organo / di Antonio Reggio.*
Material:	Manuscript: score: 4f.

Incipits:

1.1.1 S 1, 3/4 Andante; G major

Tantum ergo, sacramentum

Library:	Santini-Sammlung, Diözesanbibliothek, Münster
Siglum/ signature:	(D-MÜs/ SANT Hs 3381)

Notes:
Manuscript not in Reggio's hand

La Gelosia

Catalogue No:	Hr 21
Date:	1756
Key:	A Major
Scoring Note:	Soprano, violin 1, violin 2, viola
Language:	Italian
Genre:	Cantatas

Source description:

Original title: *Cantata a Voce sola di Soprano / per la Sig.ra Marchesa Marianna Vrigo / [at head:] A[nno] 1756 / [right at head:] Originale di Ant° Reggio*

Material: Manuscript, Autograph, score: 24f.

Incipits:

1.1.1 violin 1, c Introduzione. Con spirito grande; D major

1.2.1 Soprano, c [Recitative].;

Perdono amata Nice

1.3.1 Soprano, 3/4 [Aria]. Amoroso; G major

Bei labbri che Amore

Library: Santini-Sammlung, Diözesanbibliothek, Münster

Siglum/ signature: D-MÜs/ SANT Hs 3385 (Nr. 2)

Notes:
Dedicatee: Vrigo, Marianna, Text: Pietro Metastasio

Le Grazie vendicate

Catalogue No:	Hr 22
Date:	1763
Key:	C Major
Scoring:	Soprano (2), Alto, violin 1, violin 2, viola, basso continuo
Text:	Metastasio, Pietro
Language:	Italian
Genre:	Cantatas

Source description:

Original title: *Le Grazie Vendicate / Cantata a 3 Voci / [right at head:] Originale di Anto Reggio / A[nno] 1763.*

Material: Manuscript, Autograph score: 35f.

Incipits:

1.1.1 Soprano, c Eufrosine; [Recitative].;

Non sperate placarmi

1.2.1 violin 1, 3/8 [Aria].; F major

1.2.2 Soprano, 3/8 Eufrosine; F major

No di tanto orgoglio mi voglio vendicar

Library: Santini-Sammlung, Diözesanbibliothek, Münster

Siglum/ signature: D-MÜs/ SANT Hs 3385 (Nr. 1)

Notes:
Date in title: 1763, Date at the end: "4 Luglio 1762"

Se del fiume altera l'onda

Catalogue No:	Hr 23
Date:	1764
Key:	G major
Scoring:	Soprano, violin 1, violin 2, viola, bass
Text:	Metastasio, Pietro
Language:	Italian
Genre:	Arias

Source description:

Original title:	*[heading:] Originale di Antonio Reggio A[nno] 1764 [right:] Per la Sig^{ra} Marchese Prudenza Astalli.*
Material:	Manuscript, Autograph, score: 5f.

Incipits:

1.1.1 violin 1, 3/4 [Aria]. Con brio; G major

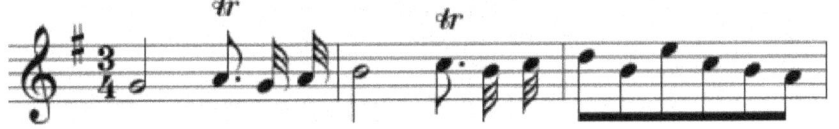

1.1.2 Soprano, 3/4 G major

Se del fiume altera l'onda

Library:	Santini-Sammlung, Diözesanbibliothek, Münster
Siglum/ signature:	D-MÜs/ SANT Hs 3385 (Nr. 4)

Notes:
Dedicatee: Astalli, Prudenza
Text is from Pietro Metastasio's "Artaserse" Scene VII, Act 2

Mio ben ricordati

Catalogue No:	Hr 24
Date:	1764
Key:	D major
Scoring:	Alto, violin 1, violin 2, viola, bass
Text:	Metastasio, Pietro
Language:	Italian
Genre:	Arias

Source description:

Original title: [heading:] Originale di Antonio Reggio A[nno] 1764 [in margin:] per la Sig^{ra} Marchesa Giacinta Astalli.

Material: Manuscript, Autograph, score: 5f.

Incipits:

1.1.1 violin 1, 6/8 Andantino; D major

1.1.2 Alto, 6/8 Andantino; D major

Mio ben ricordati

Library: Santini-Sammlung, Diözesanbibliothek, Münster

Siglum/ signature: D-MÜs/ SANT Hs 3386

Notes:
Dedicatee: Astalli, Giacinta
Text from Pietro Metastasio's "Alessandro nell'Indie" Scene X, Act 3

Misero me qual vero aspetto

Catalogue No:	Hr 25
Date:	1765
Key:	G Major
Scoring:	Soprano, (2), violin 1, violin 2, viola, oboe (2), horn (2), basso continuo
Language:	Italian
Genre:	Cantatas
Source description:	
Original title:	*[heading:] Originale di Ant° Reggio A[nno] 1765*
Material:	Manuscript, Autograph, score: 14f.

Incipits:

1.1.1 violin 1, c Andante brioso;

1.1.2 Soprano, c Andante brioso;

Misero me qual vero aspetto

1.2.1 Soprano, c [Aria].;Dmajor

Andar vorrei ma come

Library:	Santini-Sammlung, Diözesanbibliothek, Münster
Siglum/ signature:	D-MÜs/ SANT Hs 3385 (Nr. 3)

Iube Domne benedicere

Catalogue No:	Hr 26
Date:	1766
Key:	C major
Scoring:	Soprano, organ, basso continuo: organo
Language:	Latin
Genre:	Motets

Source description:

Original title:	A[nno] 1766.
Material:	Manuscript, Autograph, score: 5f.

Incipits:

1.1.1 organ, 3/4 Larghetto; C major

1.1.2 Soprano, 3/4 Larghetto; C major

Iube Domne benedicere

Library:	Santini-Sammlung, Diözesanbibliothek, Münster
Siglum/ signature:	D-MÜs/ SANT Hs 3385 (Nr. 5)

Non temer non son più amante

Catalogue No: Hr 27
Date: 1767
Key: G major
Scoring: Soprano (3), Alto, basso continuo
Text: Metastasio, Pietro
Language: Italian
Genre: Quartets
Source description:
Original title: *[without title]*
Material: Manuscript, Autograph, score: 2f.

Incipits:
1.1.1 Soprano 1, 2/4 Andantino. G major

Non temer non son più amante

Library: a) Santini-Sammlung, Diözesanbibliothek, Münster
b) Biblioteca Nazionale di Fierenze
c) Biblioteca da Palácio Nacional da Ajuda, Lisbon

Siglum/ signature: D-MÜs/ SANT Hs 3383 (Nr. 1)
I-Fn Ms MUS 338 (No 1)
P-La 46-II-49 (1)

Notes:
Text from Pietro Metastasio's "*Antigno*" Scene XII, Act 2
Sources: Cover page of collections are annotated:
a) *Concertini a tre Soprani, e Contralto / per le Signore Marchesine / Laura, Prudenza, e Giacinta Astalli / [left at head:] A[nno] 1767 / [right at head:] Originale di Ant[onio] Reggio.*
b) *Concerti A' Quattro per Trè Soprani e Contralto di Monsignor Antonino Reggio.*
c) *Concertini per Camera a Quattro Voci e Basso consagrati alla Maesta Fedelissima di Giuseppe Re di Portogallo e Algavia.*

Tu vuoi ch'io viva o cara

Catalogue No:	Hr 28
Date:	1767
Key:	G major
Scoring:	Soprano (3), Alto, basso continuo
Text:	Metastasio, Pietro
Language:	Italian
Genre:	Quartets
Source description:	
Original title:	*II. / Tu vuoi ch'io viva o Cara*
Material:	Manuscript, Autograph , score: 4f.

Incipits:

1.1.1 Soprano 1, 3/4 Andantino; G major

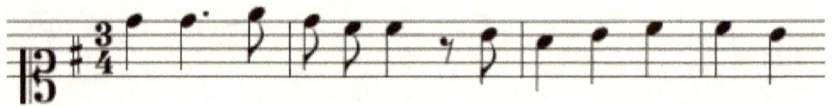

Tu vuoi ch'io viva o cara

Library:	a) Santini-Sammlung, Diözesanbibliothek, Münster
	b) Biblioteca Nazionale di Fierenze
	c) Biblioteca da Palácio Nacionale da Ajuda, Lisbon
Siglum/ signature:	D-MÜs/ SANT Hs 3383 (Nr. 2)
	I-Fn Ms MUS 338 (No 2)
	P-La 46-II-49 (2)

Notes:
Text from Pietro Metastasio's "*Artaserse*", Scene VII, Act 3
Sources: Cover page of collections are annotated:
a)   *Concertini a tre Soprani, e Contralto / per le Signore Marchesine / Laura, Prudenza, e Giacinta Astalli / [left at head:] A[nno] 1767 / [right at head:] Originale di Ant[onio] Reggio.*
b)   *Concerti A' Quattro per Trè Soprani e Contralto di Monsignor Antonino Reggio.*
c)   *Concertini per Camera a Quattro Voci e Basso consagrati alla Maesta Fedelissima di Giuseppe Re di Portogallo e Algavia.*

Ne' giorni tuoi felici

Catalogue No:	Hr 29
Date:	1767
Key:	B♭ major
Scoring:	Soprano (3), Alto, basso continuo
Text:	Metastasio, Pietro
Language:	Italian
Genre:	Quartets
Source description:	
Original title:	*III. / Ne giorni tuoi felici.*
Material:	Manuscript, Autograph, score: 4f.

Incipits:

1.1.1 Soprano 1, c/ Moderato; B♭ major

Ne' giorni tuoi felici

Library:	a) Santini-Sammlung, Diözesanbibliothek, Münster
	b) Biblioteca Nazionale di Fierenze
	c) Biblioteca da Palácio Nacional da Ajuda, Lisbon
Siglum/ signature:	D-MÜs/ SANT Hs 3383 (Nr. 3)
	I-Fn Ms MUS 338 (No 3)
	P-La 46-II-49 (3)

Notes:
Text from Pietro Metastasio's "Olimpiade" Scene X, Act 1

Sources: Cover page of collections are annotated:
a)   *Concertini a tre Soprani, e Contralto / per le Signore Marchesine / Laura, Prudenza, e Giacinta Astalli / [left at head:] A[nno] 1767 / [right at head:] Originale di Ant[onio] Reggio.*
b)   *Concerti A' Quattro per Trè Soprani e Contralto di Monsignor Antonino Reggio.*
c)   *Concertini per Camera a Quattro Voci e Basso consagrati alla Maesta Fedelissima di Giuseppe Re di Portogallo e Algavia.*

La destra ti chiedo

Catalogue No:	Hr 30
Date:	1767
Key:	G minor
Scoring:	Soprano (3), Alto, basso continuo
Text:	Metastasio, Pietro
Language:	Italian
Genre:	Quartets

Source description:

Original title:	*IV. / La destra ti chiedo*
Material:	Manuscript, Autograph, score: 4f.

Incipits:

1.1.1 Soprano 1, 2/4 Andante; G minor

La destra ti chiedo

Library:	a) Santini-Sammlung, Diözesanbibliothek, Münster
	b) Biblioteca Nazionale di Fierenze
	c) Biblioteca da Palácio Nacional da Ajuda, Lisbon
Siglum/ signature:	D-MÜs/ SANT Hs 3383 (Nr. 4)
	I-Fn Ms MUS 338 (No 4)
	P-La 46-II-49 (4)

Notes:
Text from Pietro Metastasio's "*Demofoonte*", Scene XI, Act 2

Sources: Cover page of collections are annotated:
a) *Concertini a tre Soprani, e Contralto / per le Signore Marchesine / Laura, Prudenza, e Giacinta Astalli / [left at head:] A[nno] 1767 / [right at head:] Originale di Ant[onio] Reggio.*
b) *Concerti A' Quattro per Trè Soprani e Contralto di Monsignor Antonino Reggio.*
c) *Concertini per Camera a Quattro Voci e Basso consagrati alla Maesta Fedelissima di Giuseppe Re di Portogallo e Algavia.*

Sì ti credo amato bene

Catalogue No:	Hr 31
Date:	1767
Key:	A major
Scoring:	Soprano (3), Alto, basso continuo
Text:	Metastasio, Pietro
Language:	Italian
Genre:	Quartets
Source description:	
Original title:	V. / *Si ti credo amato Bene.*
Material:	Manuscript, Autograph, score: 4f.
Incipits:	

1.1.1 Soprano 1, 2/4 Andante; A major

Sì ti credo amato bene

Library:	a) Santini-Sammlung, Diözesanbibliothek, Münster
	b) Biblioteca Nazionale di Fierenze
	c) Biblioteca da Palácio Nacional da Ajuda, Lisbon
Siglum/ signature:	D-MÜs/ SANT Hs 3383 (Nr. 5)
	I-Fn Ms MUS 338 (No 5)
	P-La 46-II-49 (5)

Notes:
Text from Pietro Metastasio's "*Nitteti*", Scene X, Act 1

Sources: Cover page of collections are annotated:
a) *Concertini a tre Soprani, e Contralto / per le Signore Marchesine / Laura, Prudenza, e Giacinta Astalli / [left at head:] A[nno] 1767 / [right at head:] Originale di Ant[onio] Reggio.*
b) *Concerti A' Quattro per Tré Soprani e Contralto di Monsignor Antonino Reggio.*
c) *Concertini per Camera a Quattro Voci e Basso consagrati alla Maesta Fedelissima di Giuseppe Re di Portogallo e Algavia.*

Mille volte o mio tesoro

Catalogue No:	Hr 32
Date:	1767
Key:	G major
Scoring:	Soprano (3), Alto, basso continuo
Text:	Metastasio, Pietro
Language:	Italian
Genre:	Quartets

Source description:

Original title:	*VI. / Mille volte o mio Tesoro.*
Material:	Manuscript, Autograph, score: 3f.

Incipits:

1.1.1 Soprano 1, c/ Allegretto; G major

Mille volte o mio tesoro

Library:	a) Santini-Sammlung, Diözesanbibliothek, Münster
	b) Biblioteca Nazionale di Fierenze
	c) Biblioteca da Palácio Nacional da Ajuda, Lisbon
Siglum/ signature:	D-MÜs/ SANT Hs 3383 (Nr. 6)
	I-Fn Ms MUS 338 (No 6)
	P-La 46-II-49 (6)

Notes:
Text from Pietro Metastasio's "*La Danza*"

Sources: Cover page of collections are annotated:
a) *Concertini a tre Soprani, e Contralto / per le Signore Marchesine / Laura, Prudenza, e Giacinta Astalli / [left at head:] A[nno] 1767 / [right at head:] Originale di Ant[onio] Reggio.*
b) *Concerti A' Quattro per Trè Soprani e Contralto di Monsignor Antonino Reggio.*
c) *Concertini per Camera a Quattro Voci e Basso consagrati alla Maesta Fedelissima di Giuseppe Re di Portogallo e Algavia.*

Va ti consola addio

Catalogue No:	Hr 33
Date:	1767
Key:	D major
Scoring:	Soprano (3), Alto, basso continuo
Text:	Metastasio, Pietro
Language:	Italian
Genre:	Quartets
Source description:	
Original title:	*VII. / Và ti consola addio.*
Material:	Manuscript, Autograph, score: 4f.

Incipits:

1.1.1 Soprano 1, 3/4 Andante; D major

Va ti consola addio

Library:	a) Santini-Sammlung, Diözesanbibliothek, Münster
	b) Biblioteca Nazionale di Fierenze
	c) Biblioteca da Palácio Nacional da Ajuda, Lisbon
Siglum/ signature:	D-MÜs/ SANT Hs 3383 (Nr. 7)
	I-Fn Ms MUS 338 (No 7)
	P-La 46-II-49 (7)

Notes:
Text from Pietro Metastasio's "*Zenobia*", Scene III, Act 2

Sources: Cover page of collections are annotated:
a) *Concertini a tre Soprani, e Contralto / per le Signore Marchesine / Laura, Prudenza, e Giacinta Astalli / [left at head:] A[nno] 1767 / [right at head:] Originale di Ant[onio] Reggio.*
b) *Concerti A' Quattro per Trè Soprani e Contralto di Monsignor Antonino Reggio.*
c) *Concertini per Camera a Quattro Voci e Basso consagrati alla Maestà Fedelissima di Giuseppe Re di Portogallo e Algavia.*

Ah se di te mi privi

Catalogue No:	Hr 34
Date:	1767
Key:	F major
Scoring:	Soprano (3), Alto, basso continuo
Text:	Metastasio, Pietro
Language:	Italian
Genre:	Quartets
Source description:	
Original title:	*VIII. / Ah se di te mi privi*
Material:	Manuscript, Autograph, score: 4f.

Incipits:

1.1.1 Soprano 1, c Larghetto; F major

Ah se di te mi privi

Library:	a) Santini-Sammlung, Diözesanbibliothek, Münster
	b) Biblioteca Nazionale di Fierenze
	c) Biblioteca da Palácio Nacional da Ajuda, Lisbon
Siglum/ signature:	D-MÜs/ SANT Hs 3383 (Nr. 8)
	I-Fn Ms MUS 338 (No 8)
	P-La 46-II-49 (8)

Notes:
Text from Pietro Metastasio's "*Impermestrà*", Scene X, Act 2 (See Hr 45)

Sources: Cover page of collections are annotated:
a) *Concertini a tre Soprani, e Contralto / per le Signore Marchesine / Laura, Prudenza, e Giacinta Astalli / [left at head:] A[nno] 1767 / [right at head:] Originale di Ant[onio] Reggio.*
b) *Concerti A' Quattro per Trè Soprani e Contralto di Monsignor Antonino Reggio.*
c) *Concertini per Camera a Quattro Voci e Basso consagrati alla Maesta Fedelissima di Giuseppe Re di Portogallo e Algavia.*

Crudel morir mi vedi

Catalogue No:	Hr 35
Date:	1767
Key:	B♭ major
Scoring:	Soprano (3), Alto, basso continuo
Text:	Metastasio, Pietro
Language:	Italian
Genre:	Quartets

Source description:

Original title:	*IX. / Crudel morir mi vedi.*
Material:	Manuscript, Autograph, score: 4f.

Incipits:

1.1.1 Soprano 1, c/ Allegro; B♭ major

Crudel morir mi vedi

Library:	a) Santini-Sammlung, Diözesanbibliothek, Münster
	b) Biblioteca Nazionale di Fierenze
	c) Biblioteca da Palácio Nacional da Ajuda, Lisbon
Siglum/ signature:	D-MÜs/ SANT Hs 3383 (Nr. 9)
	I-Fn Ms MUS 338 (No 9)
	P-La 46-II-49 (9)

Notes:
Text from Pietro Metastasio's "Semiramide", Scene X, Act 2

Sources: Cover page of collections are annotated:
a) *Concertini a tre Soprani, e Contralto / per le Signore Marchesine / Laura, Prudenza, e Giacinta Astalli / [left at head:] A[nno] 1767 / [right at head:] Originale di Ant[onio] Reggio.*
b) *Concerti A' Quattro per Trè Soprani e Contralto di Monsignor Antonino Reggio.*
c) *Concertini per Camera a Quattro Voci e Basso consagrati alla Maesta Fedelissima di Giuseppe Re di Portogallo e Algavia.*

Se mai turbo il tuo riposo

Catalogue No:	Hr 36
Date:	1767
Key:	A major
Scoring:	Soprano (3), Alto, basso continuo
Text:	Metastasio, Pietro
Language:	Italian
Genre:	Quartets

Source description:

Original title:	X. / *Se mai turbo il tuo riposo.*
Material:	Manuscript, Autograph, score: 4f.

Incipits:

1.1.1 Soprano 1, c Andante; A major

Se mai turbo il tuo riposo

Library:	a) Santini-Sammlung, Diözesanbibliothek, Münster
	b) Biblioteca Nazionale di Fierenze
	c) Biblioteca da Palácio Nacional da Ajuda, Lisbon
Siglum/ signature:	D-MÜs/ SANT Hs 3383 (Nr.10)
	I-Fn Ms MUS 338 (No 10)
	P-La 46-II-49 (10)

Notes:
Text from Pietro Metastasio's "Alessandro nell.Indie", Scene XVI, Act 1

Sources: Cover page of collections are annotated:
a) *Concertini a tre Soprani, e Contralto / per le Signore Marchesine / Laura, Prudenza, e Giacinta Astalli / [left at head:] A[nno] 1767 / [right at head:] Originale di Ant[onio] Reggio.*
b) *Concerti A' Quattro per Trè Soprani e Contralto di Monsignor Antonino Reggio.*
c) *Concertini per Camera a Quattro Voci e Basso consagrati alla Maestà Fedelissima di Giuseppe Re di Portogallo e Algavia.*

Vanne a regnar ben mio

Catalogue No:	Hr 37
Date:	1767
Key:	C major
Scoring:	Soprano (3), Alto, basso continuo
Text:	Metastasio, Pietro
Language:	Italian
Genre:	Quartets
Source description:	
Original title:	*XI. / Vanne a regnar Ben mio.*
Material:	Manuscript, Autograph, score: 4f.

Incipits:

1.1.1 Soprano 1, 3/4 Allegretto amoroso; C major

Vanne a regnar ben mio

Library:	a) Santini-Sammlung, Diözesanbibliothek, Münster
	b) Biblioteca Nazionale di Fierenze
	c) Biblioteca da Palácio Nacional da Ajuda, Lisbon
Siglum/ signature:	D-MÜs/ SANT Hs 3383 (Nr.11)
	I-Fn Ms MUS 338 (No 11)
	P-La 46-II-49 (11)

Notes:
Text from Pietro Metastasio's "Il re patore" Scene VIII, Act 1

Sources: Cover page of collections are annotated:
a) *Concertini a tre Soprani, e Contralto / per le Signore Marchesine / Laura, Prudenza, e Giacinta Astalli / [left at head:] A[nno] 1767 / [right at head:] Originale di Ant[onio] Reggio.*
b) *Concerti A' Quattro per Trè Soprani e Contralto di Monsignor Antonino Reggio.*
c) *Concertini per Camera a Quattro Voci e Basso consagrati alla Maestà Fedelissima di Giuseppe Re di Portogallo e Algavia.*

Ah che vuol dir quel pianto

Catalogue No:	Hr 38
Date:	1767
Key:	E♭ major
Scoring:	Soprano (3), Alto, basso continuo
Text:	Metastasio, Pietro
Language:	Italian
Genre:	Quartets

Source description:

Original title:	*XII. / Ah che vuol dir quel pianto.*
Material:	Manuscript, Autograph, score: 4f.

Incipits:

1.1.1 Soprano 1, c/ Larghetto; E♭major

Ah che vuol dir quel pianto

Library:	a) Santini-Sammlung, Diözesanbibliothek, Münster
	b) Biblioteca Nazionale di Fierenze
	c) Biblioteca da Palácio Nacional da Ajuda, Lisbon
Siglum/ signature:	D-MÜs/ SANT Hs 3383 (Nr.12)
	I-Fn Ms MUS 338 (No 12)
	P-La 46-II-49 (12)

Notes:
Text from Pietro Metastasio's "*Romolo ed Ersilia*" Scene IV, Act 1

Sources: Cover page of collections are annotated:
a)   *Concertini a tre Soprani, e Contralto / per le Signore Marchesine / Laura, Prudenza, e Giacinta Astalli / [left at head:] A[nno] 1767 / [right at head:] Originale di Ant[onio] Reggio.*
b)   *Concerti A' Quattro per Trè Soprani e Contralto di Monsignor Antonino Reggio.*
c)   *Concertini per Camera a Quattro Voci e Basso consagrati alla Maesta Fedelissima di Giuseppe Re di Portogallo e Algavia.*

Sì ti fido al tuo gran core

Catalogue No: Hr 39
Date: 1767
Key: E major
Scoring: Soprano (3), Alto, basso continuo
Text: Metastasio, Pietro
Language: Italian
Genre: Quartets
Source description:
Original title: *XIII. / Sì ti fido al tuo gran core.*
Material: Manuscript, Autograph, score: 4f.
Incipits:

1.1.1 Soprano 1, c Allegro; E major

Sì ti fido al tuo gran core

Library: a) Santini-Sammlung, Diözesanbibliothek, Münster
b) Biblioteca Nazionale di Fierenze
c) Biblioteca da Palácio Nacional da Ajuda, Lisbon
Siglum/ signature: D-MÜs/ SANT Hs 3383 (Nr.13)
I-Fn Ms MUS 338 (No 13)
P-La 46-II-49 (13)
Notes:
Text from Pietro Metastasio's "Il trionfo di Clelia" Scene III. Act 2

Sources: Cover page of collections are annotated:
a) *Concertini a tre Soprani, e Contralto / per le Signore Marchesine / Laura, Prudenza, e Giacinta Astalli / [left at head:] A[nno] 1767 / [right at head:] Originale di Ant[onio] Reggio.*
b) *Concerti A' Quattro per Trè Soprani e Contralto di Monsignor Antonino Reggio.*
c) *Concertini per Camera a Quattro Voci e Basso consagrati alla Maesta Fedelissima di Giuseppe Re di Portogallo e Algavia.*

Sappi ch'al nascer mio

Catalogue No:	Hr 40
Date:	1767
Key:	A major
Scoring:	Soprano (3), Alto, basso continuo
Text:	Metastasio, Pietro
Language:	Italian
Genre:	Quartets

Source description:

Original title:	*XIV. / Sappi ch'al nascer mio.*
Material:	Manuscript, Autograph, score: 4f.

Incipits:

1.1.1 Soprano 1, c Andante; A major

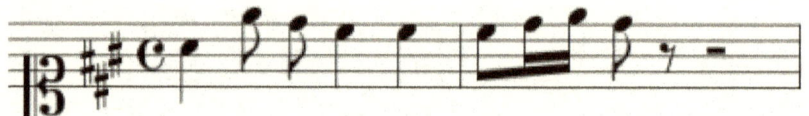

Sappi ch'al nascer mio

Library:	a) Santini-Sammlung, Diözesanbibliothek, Münster
	b) Biblioteca Nazionale di Fierenze
	c) Biblioteca da Palácio Nacional da Ajuda, Lisbon
Siglum/ signature:	D-MÜs/ SANT Hs 3383 (Nr.14)
	I-Fn Ms MUS 338 (No 14)
	P-La 46-II-49 (14)

Notes:
Text from Pietro Metastasio's "Ciro riconosciuto" Scene XIII, Act 1

Sources: Cover page of collections are annotated:
a) *Concertini a tre Soprani, e Contralto / per le Signore Marchesine / Laura, Prudenza, e Giacinta Astalli / [left at head:] A[nno] 1767 / [right at head:] Originale di Ant[onio] Reggio.*
b) *Concerti A' Quattro per Trè Soprani e Contralto di Monsignor Antonino Reggio.*
c) *Concertini per Camera a Quattro Voci e Basso consagrati alla Maesta Fedelissima di Giuseppe Re di Portogallo e Algavia.*

Perché se re tu sei

Catalogue No:	Hr 41
Date:	1767
Key:	B♭ major
Scoring:	Soprano (3), Alto, basso continuo
Text:	Metastasio, Pietro
Language:	Italian
Genre:	Quartets
Source description:	
Original title:	*XV. / Perchè se Re tu sei.*
Material:	Manuscript, Autograph, score: 4f.

Incipits:

1.1.1 Soprano 1, 3/4 Andante; B♭major

Perché se re tu sei

Library:	a) Santini-Sammlung, Diözesanbibliothek, Münster
	b) Biblioteca Nazionale di Fierenze
	c) Biblioteca da Palácio Nacional da Ajuda, Lisbon
Siglum/ signature:	D-MÜs/ SANT Hs 3383 (Nr. 15)
	I-Fn Ms MUS 338 (No 15)
	P-La 46-II-49 (15)

Notes:

Text from Pietro Metastasio's "L'Eroe cinese" Scene VIII, Act 2

Sources: Cover page of collections are annotated:
a) *Concertini a tre Soprani, e Contralto / per le Signore Marchesine / Laura, Prudenza, e Giacinta Astalli / [left at head:] A[nno] 1767 / [right at head:] Originale di Ant[onio] Reggio.*
b) *Concerti A' Quattro per Trè Soprani e Contralto di Monsignor Antonino Reggio.*
c) *Concertini per Camera a Quattro Voci e Basso consagrati alla Maestà Fedelissima di Giuseppe Re di Portogallo e Algavia.*

Cara non tanto sdegno

Catalogue No:	Hr 42
Date:	1767
Key:	C minor
Scoring:	Soprano (3), Alto, basso continuo
Language:	Italian
Genre:	Quartets
Source description:	
Original title:	*XVI. / Cara non tanto sdegno.*
Material:	Manuscript, Autograph , score: 4f.

Incipits:

1.1.1 Soprano 1, 3/4 Adagio; C minor

Cara non tanto sdegno

Library:	a) Santini-Sammlung, Diözesanbibliothek, Münster
	b) Biblioteca Nazionale di Fierenze
	c) Biblioteca da Palácio Nacional da Ajuda, Lisbon
Siglum/ signature:	D-MÜs/ SANT Hs 3383 (Nr.16)
	I-Fn Ms MUS 338 (No 16)
	P-La 46-II-49 (16)

Notes:

Sources: Cover page of collections are annotated:
a)   *Concertini a tre Soprani, e Contralto / per le Signore Marchesine / Laura, Prudenza, e Giacinta Astalli / [left at head:] A[nno] 1767 / [right at head:] Originale di Ant[onio] Reggio.*
b)   *Concerti A' Quattro per Trè Soprani e Contralto di Monsignor Antonino Reggio.*
c)   *Concertini per Camera a Quattro Voci e Basso consagrati alla Maesta Fedelissima di Giuseppe Re di Portogallo e Algavia.*

L'estremo pegno almeno

Catalogue No:	Hr 43
Date:	1767
Key:	F major
Scoring:	Soprano (3), Alto, basso continuo
Text:	[Metastasio, Pietro]
Language:	Italian
Genre:	Quartets

Source description:

Original title:	*XVII. / L'estremo pegno almeno.*
Material:	Manuscript, Autograph, score: 4f.

Incipits:

1.1.1 Soprano 1, 12/8 Siciliana; F major

L'estremo pegno almeno

Library:	a) Santini-Sammlung, Diözesanbibliothek, Münster
	b) Biblioteca Nazionale di Fierenze
	c) Biblioteca da Palácio Nacional da Ajuda, Lisbon
Siglum/ signature:	D-MÜs/ SANT Hs 3383 (Nr.17)
	I-Fn Ms MUS 338 (No 17)
	P-La 46-II-49 (17)

Notes:

Text from Giovanni Battista Pergolesi, "*Adriano in Siria*" Act 3

Sources: Cover page of collections are annotated:
a)   *Concertini a tre Soprani, e Contralto / per le Signore Marchesine / Laura, Prudenza, e Giacinta Astalli / [left at head:] A[nno] 1767 / [right at head:] Originale di Ant[onio] Reggio.*
b)   *Concerti A' Quattro per Trè Soprani e Contralto di Monsignor Antonino Reggio.*
c)   *Concertini per Camera a Quattro Voci e Basso consagrati alla Maesta Fedelissima di Giuseppe Re di Portogallo e Algavia.*

Scocca o cielo ardenti strali

Catalogue No:	Hr 44
Date:	1767
Key:	E♭ major
Scoring:	Soprano (3), Alto, basso continuo
Language:	Italian
Genre:	Quartets

Source description:

Original title:	*XVIII. / Scocca o Cielo ardenti strali.*
Material:	Manuscript, Autograph, score: 4f.

Incipits:

1.1.1 Soprano 1, c Allegro; E♭ major

Scocca o cielo ardenti strali

Library:	a) Santini-Sammlung, Diözesanbibliothek, Münster
	b) Biblioteca Nazionale di Fierenze
	c) Biblioteca da Palácio Nacional da Ajuda, Lisbon
Siglum/ signature:	D-MÜs/ SANT Hs 3383 (Nr.18)
	I-Fn Ms MUS 338 (No 18)
	P-La 46-II-49 (18)

Notes:

Sources: Cover page of collections are annotated:
a) *Concertini a tre Soprani, e Contralto / per le Signore Marchesine / Laura, Prudenza, e Giacinta Astalli / [left at head:] A[nno] 1767 / [right at head:] Originale di Ant[onio] Reggio.*
b) *Concerti A' Quattro per Trè Soprani e Contralto di Monsignor Antonino Reggio.*
c) *Concertini per Camera a Quattro Voci e Basso consagrati alla Maesta Fedelissima di Giuseppe Re di Portogallo e Algavia.*

Ah se di te mi privi

Catalogue No:	Hr 45
Date:	1767
Key:	G minor
Scoring:	Soprano (3), Alto, basso continuo
Text:	Metastasio, Pietro
Language:	Italian
Genre:	Quartets

Source description:

Original title:	*Ah se di te mi privi.*
Material:	Manuscript, Autograph, score: 4f.

Incipits:

1.1.1 Soprano 1, 3/4 Andantino; G minor

Ah se di te mi privi

Library:	a) Santini-Sammlung, Diözesanbibliothek, Münster
	b) Biblioteca Nazionale di Fierenze
	c) Biblioteca da Palácio Nacional da Ajuda, Lisbon
Siglum/ signature:	D-MÜs/ SANT Hs 3383 (Nr.19)
	I-Fn Ms MUS 338 (No 19)
	P-La 46-II-49 (19)

Notes:
Text from Pietro Metastasio's "Impermestra" SceneX, Act 2 Different setting of Hr 34

Sources: Cover page of collections are annotated:
a) *Concertini a tre Soprani, e Contralto / per le Signore Marchesine / Laura, Prudenza, e Giacinta Astalli / [left at head:] A[nno] 1767 / [right at head:] Originale di Ant[onio] Reggio.*
b) *Concerti A' Quattro per Trè Soprani e Contralto di Monsignor Antonino Reggio.*
c) *Concertini per Camera a Quattro Voci e Basso consagrati alla Maesta Fedelissima di Giuseppe Re di Portogallo e Algavia.*

Io scordarmi il mio diletto

Catalogue No:	Hr 46
Date:	1767
Key:	G major
Scoring:	Soprano (3), Alto, basso continuo
Text:	Metastasio, Pietro
Language:	Italian
Genre:	Quartets

Source description:

Original title: *XX Io scordarmi il mio Diletto.*

Material: Manuscript, Autograph, score: 4f.

Incipits:

1.1.1 Soprano 1, c Andante molto; G major

Io scordarmi il mio diletto

Library: a) Santini-Sammlung, Diözesanbibliothek, Münster
b) Biblioteca Nazionale di Fierenze
c) Biblioteca da Palácio Nacional da Ajuda, Lisbon

Siglum/ signature: D-MÜs SANT Hs 3383 (Nr. 20)
I-Fn Ms MUS 338 (No 20)
P-La 46-II-49 (20)

Notes:
Text from Pietro Metastasio's "Partenope" Scene XI, Act 1.

Sources: Cover page of collections are annotated:
a)   *Concertini a tre Soprani, e Contralto / per le Signore Marchesine / Laura, Prudenza, e Giacinta Astalli / [left at head:] A[nno] 1767 / [right at head:] Originale di Ant[onio] Reggio.*
b)   *Concerti A' Quattro per Trè Soprani e Contralto di Monsignor Antonino Reggio.*
c)   *Concertini per Camera a Quattro Voci e Basso consagrati alla Maesta Fedelissima di Giuseppe Re di Portogallo e Algavia.*

Il Re Mesa

Catalogue No:	Hr Misc 1
Date:	1750
Genre:	Azione Sacra
Source description:	
Original title:	*Il rè Mesa. Azione sacra da cantarsi nella chiesa del venerabile monastero di S. Niccolo l'Arena di questa chiarissima, e fedelissima città di Catania per la solennità del S. Chiodo consecrata al revendissimo padre d.Idelfonzo Arezzi abate de' monasterj di S. Maria di Licodia, e di S. Niccol• l'Arena. Musica del signor d. Antonino Reggio dei principi di Campofiorito'*
Material:	Monograph, Printed text, p 40
Library:	*Biblioteca Centrale della Regione Siciliana* Palermo
Siglum/ signature:	I-PLn, Misc. A. 234 132734

Notes:
In Catania : nel Palazzo dell'Illmo Senato stamperia del dottor Bisagni, 1750 - Palermo -

II Keyboard Sonatas

1. Index by Key

1. Index by Key:

C Major	Hr 49 Hr 61 Hr 74 Hr 88 Hr 101 Hr 103 Hr 112
C minor	Hr 54 Hr 81 Hr 87 Hr 94 Hr 113
D Major	Hr 56 Hr 69 Hr 77 Hr 89 Hr 104 Hr 109
D minor	Hr 65 Hr 102
E Major	Hr 58 Hr 66 Hr 85 Hr 117
E♭ Major	Hr 53 Hr 75 HR 76 Hr 99 Hr 107 Hr 110
E Minor	Hr 72
E♭ minor	Hr 78
F Major	Hr 50 Hr 59 Hr 80 Hr 83 Hr 96 Hr 108 Hr 116
F♯ Major	Hr 93
F minor	Hr 68 Hr 115
F♯ minor	Hr 90
G Major	Hr 47 Hr 55 Hr 64 Hr 79 Hr 91 Hr 95 Hr 111
G minor	Hr 57 Hr 76 Hr 100
A♭ Major	Hr 67
A Major	Hr 52 Hr 63 Hr 82 Hr 84 Hr 98 Hr 114
A minor	Hr 51
B Major	Hr 73
B minor	Hr 60
B♭ Major	Hr 48 Hr 70 Hr 71 Hr 86 Hr 97 Hr 105 Hr 106
B♭ minor	Hr 62

Sonata in G major

Catalogue No:	Hr 47
Date:	[n.d.]
Key:	G major
Scoring:	cembalo
Genre:	Keyboard Sonatas

Source description

Original title:	Sonata Prima.
Material:	Manuscript, Autograph, 1 parts: 6f.

Incipits

1.1.1 cemb, c Allegro assai e brioso; G major

1.2.1 cemb, 2/4 Andante staccato; D major

1.3.1 cemb, 6/8 Allegro; G major

Library:	a) Santini-Sammlung, Diözesanbibliothek, Münster b) Monumento Nazionale di Montecassino, Biblioteca c) Staatsbibliothek zu Berlin - Preußischer Kulturbesitz, Musikabteilung, Berlin
Siglum/ signature:	D-MÜs/ SANT Hs 3389 (Nr. 1) I-MC/ 6-F-8/6a D-B/ Mus.ms. 18165 (f7v-8r)

Notes:
a) Title Page of collection: *Sonate per Cembalo di Ant° Reggio / Opera Prima / [left at head:] Originale*
b) Title on Manuscript: *Suonate Per Cembalo del Sig. D. Antonio Reggio*
c) This manuscript contains only the 2nd movement.

Sonata in B♭ major

Catalogue No: Hr 48
Date: [n.d.]
Key: B♭ major
Scoring: cembalo
Genre: Keyboard Sonatas
Source description
Original title: Sonata Seconda.
Material: Manuscript, Autograph, 1 parts: 5f.

Incipits: (D-MÜs/ SANT Hs 3389)
1.1.1 cemb, c Andante; B♭ major

1.2.1 cemb, 3/4 Minué. Allegro; B♭ major

Incipit: (I-MC/ 6-F-8/6b)

Library: a) Santini-Sammlung, Diözesanbibliothek, Münster
b) Monumento Nazionale di Montecassino, Biblioteca

Siglum/ signature: D-MÜs/ SANT Hs 3389 (Nr. 2)
I-MC/ 6-F-8/6b

Notes:
Literature: *The Breitkopf Thematic Catalogue. The six parts and sixteen supplements 1762-1787*, suppl.7: 1772, clm.473 (New York, 1966)
"*IV Sonate di Antonio Reggio, a cembalo Solo Amsterd.*" (II)

a) Title Page of collection: *Sonate per Cembalo di Ant° Reggio / Opera Prima / [left at head:] Originale*

Sonata in C major

Catalogue No:	Hr 49
Date:	[n.d.]
Key:	C major
Scoring :	cembalo
Genre:	Keyboard Sonatas

Source description

Original title:	Sonata Terza.
Material:	Manuscript, Autograph, 1 parts: 6f

Incipits

1.1.1 cemb, c Allegro; C major

1.2.1 cemb, 6/8 Larghetto; C minor

1.3.1 cemb, 3/8 Allegro; C major

Library:	a) Santini-Sammlung, Diözesanbibliothek, Münster
	b) Monumento Nazionale di Montecassino, Biblioteca
	c) Staatsbibliothek zu Berlin - Preußischer Kulturbesitz, Musikabteilung, Berlin
Siglum/ signature:	D-MÜs/ SANT Hs 3389 (Nr. 3)
	I-MC/ 6-F-8/6c
	D-B/ Mus.ms. 18165 (f8v-10r)

Notes:
Literature: *The Breitkopf Thematic Catalogue. The six parts and sixteen supplements 1762-1787,* suppl.7: 1772, clm.473 (New York, 1966)
"*IV Sonate di Antonio Reggio, a cembalo Solo Amsterd.*" (V)

a) Title Page of collection: *Sonate per Cembalo di Ant° Reggio / Opera Prima / [left at head:] Originale*
b) Second movement in I-MC/ 6-F-8/6c shown as G minor.
c) This manuscript only contains 3rd movement.

Sonata in F major

Catalogue No: Hr 50
Date: [n.d.]
Key: F major
Scoring: cembalo
Genre: Keyboard Sonatas

Source description
Original title: Sonata Quarta.
Material: Manuscript, Autograph, 1 parts: 6f

Incipits (D-MÜs/ SANT Hs 3389)

1.1.1 cemb, c Allegro assai; F major

1.2.1 cemb, 3/4 Andantino; F minor

1.3.1 cemb, 3/8 Allegro; F major

Incipit (I-MC/6-f-8/3a)

Library: a) Santini-Sammlung, Diözesanbibliothek, Münster
b) Monumento Nazionale di Montecassino, Biblioteca

Siglum/ signature: D-MÜs/ SANT Hs 3389 (Nr. 4)
I-MC/ 6-F-8/3a

Notes:
a) Title Page of collection: *Sonate per Cembalo di Ant° Reggio / Opera Prima / [left at head:] Originale*

Sonata in A minor

Catalogue No:	Hr 51
Date:	[n.d.]
Key:	A minor
Scoring:	cembalo
Genre:	Keyboard Sonatas

Source description

Original title:	Sonata Quinta.
Material:	Manuscript, Autograph, 1 parts: 6f.

Incipits

1.1.1 cemb, 3/4 Allegro non molto; A minor

1.2.1 cemb, c/ Adagio; C major

1.3.1 cemb, 3/4 Presto; A minor

Library:	a) Santini-Sammlung, Diözesanbibliothek, Münster
	b) Monumento Nazionale di Montecassino, Biblioteca
	c) Staatsbibliothek zu Berlin - Preußischer Kulturbesitz, Musikabteilung, Berlin
Siglum/ signature:	D-MÜs/ SANT Hs 3389 (Nr. 5)
	I-MC/ 6-F-8/3b
	D-B/ Mus.ms. 18165 (f10v-12r)

Notes:
a) Title Page of collection: *Sonate per Cembalo di Ant° Reggio / Opera Prima / [left at head:] Originale*
c) This manuscript contains only the 3rd movement.

Sonata in A major

Catalogue No:	Hr 52
Date:	[n.d.]
Key:	A major
Scoring:	cembalo
Genre:	Keyboard Sonatas

Source description

Original title:	Sonata Sesta.
Material:	Manuscript, Autograph, 1 parts: 6f.

Incipits

1.1.1 cemb, c Allegro; A major

1.2.1 cemb, c/ Adagio; A major

1.3.1 cemb, 3/8 Presto; A major

Library:	a) Santini-Sammlung, Diözesanbibliothek, Münster
	b) Monumento Nazionale di Montecassino, Biblioteca
	c) Staatsbibliothek zu Berlin - Preußischer Kulturbesitz, Musikabteilung, Berlin
Siglum/ signature:	D-MÜs/ SANT Hs 3389 (Nr. 6)
	I-MC/ 6-F-8/3c
	D-B/ Mus.ms. 18165 (f12v-16r)

Notes:
a) Title Page of collection: *Sonate per Cembalo di Ant° Reggio / Opera Prima / [left at head:] Originale*
b) This Manuscript contains only the 2nd and 3rd movements.

Sonata in E♭ major

Catalogue No:	Hr 53
Date:	[n.d.]
Key:	E♭ major
Scoring:	cembalo
Genre:	Keyboard Sonatas

Source description

Original title:	Sonata Settima.
Material:	Manuscript, Autograph, 1 parts: 6f

Incipits

1.1.1 cemb, c Allegro moderato; E♭ major

1.2.1 cemb, 3/4 Sostenuto; E♭ major

1.3.1 cemb, 3/8 Presto; E♭ major

Library:	a) Santini-Sammlung, Diözesanbibliothek, Münster
	b) Monumento Nazionale di Montecassino, Biblioteca
	c) Staatsbibliothek zu Berlin - Preußischer Kulturbesitz, Musikabteilung, Berlin
Siglum/ signature:	D-MÜs/ SANT Hs 3389 (Nr. 7)
	I-MC/ 6-F-8/2a
	D-B/ Mus.ms. 18165 (f16v-18r)

Notes:

Literature: *The Breitkopf Thematic Catalogue. The six parts and sixteen supplements 1762-1787,* suppl.7: 1772, clm.473 (New York, 1966)
"*IV Sonate di Antonio Reggio, a cembalo Solo Amsterd.*" (IV)

a) Title Page of collection: *Sonate per Cembalo di Ant° Reggio / Opera Prima / [left at head:] Originale*
b) Second movement of I-MC/ 6-F-8/2a: (1.2.1 3/4 Spiritoso; E♭major)
c) This Manuscript contains only the 3rd movement.

Sonata in C minor

Catalogue No: Hr 54
Date: [n.d.]
Key: C minor
Scoring: cembalo
Genre: Keyboard Sonatas
Source description
Original title: Sonata Ottava.
Material: Manuscript, Autograph 1 parts: 6f.
Incipits (D-MÜs/ SANT Hs 3389)

1.1.1 cemb, c Allegro non molto; C minor

1.2.1 cemb, c/ Cantabile; Eb major
1.3.1 cemb, 3/4 Allegro; C minor

Library: a) Santini-Sammlung, Diözesanbibliothek, Münster
b) Monumento Nazionale di Montecassino, Biblioteca

Siglum/ signature: D-MÜs/ SANT Hs 3389 (Nr. 8)
I-MC/ 6-F-8/2b

Notes
Literature: *The Breitkopf Thematic Catalogue. The six parts and sixteen supplements 1762-1787*, suppl.7: 1772, clm.473 (New York, 1966)
"*IV Sonate di Antonio Reggio, a cembalo Solo Amsterd.*" (III)

a) Title Page of collection: *Sonate per Cembalo di Ant° Reggio / Opera Prima / [left at head:] Originale*
b) Third movement of I-MC/ 6-F-8/2b: (1.3.1 2/4 Allegro; C minor)

Sonata in G major

Catalogue No:	Hr 55
Date:	[n.d.]
Key:	G major
Scoring:	cembalo
Genre:	Keyboard Sonatas

Source description

Original title:	Sonata Nona.
Material:	Manuscript, Autograph 1 parts: 6f.

Incipits

1.1.1 cemb, c/ Andante; G major

1.2.1 cemb, 3/4 Partite.; G major

Library:	a) Santini-Sammlung, Diözesanbibliothek, Münster
	b) Monumento Nazionale di Montecassino, Biblioteca
Siglum/ signature:	D-MÜs/ SANT Hs 3389 (Nr. 9)
	I-MC/ 6-F-8/2c

Notes:
a) Title Page of collection: *Sonate per Cembalo di Ant° Reggio / Opera Prima / [left at head:] Originale*

Sonata in D major

Catalogue No:	Hr 56
Date:	[n.d.]
Key:	D major
Scoring:	cembalo
Genre:	Keyboard Sonatas

Source description

Original title:	Sonata Decima.
Material:	Manuscript, Autograph, 1 parts: 5f.

Incipits

1.1.1 cemb, 3/4 Andante; D major

1.2.1 cemb, c Allegro; D major

1.3.1 cemb, 6/8 Allegro; D major

Library:	a) Santini-Sammlung, Diözesanbibliothek, Münster
	b) Monumento Nazionale di Montecassino, Biblioteca
	c) Staatsbibliothek zu Berlin - Preußischer Kulturbesitz, Musikabteilung, Berlin
Siglum/ signature:	D-MÜs/ SANT Hs 3389 (Nr. 10)
	I-MC/ 6-A-1/15a
	D-B/ Mus.ms. 18165 (f1v-7r)

Notes:

Literatur: *The Breitkopf Thematic Catalogue. The six parts and sixteen supplements 1762-1787*, suppl.7: 1772, clm.473 (New York, 1966)
   "*IV Sonate di Antonio Reggio, a cembalo Solo Amsterd.*" (VI)
a) Title Page of collection: *Sonate per Cembalo di Ant° Reggio / Opera Prima / [left at head:] Originale*
b) Additional Movement in I-MC/ 6-A-1/15a: (1.3.1 3/8 Fuga. Allegro; A minor)
c) This manuscript contains all four movements as in the I-MC version.

Sonata in G minor

Catalogue No: Hr 57
Date: [n.d.]
Key: G minor
Scoring: cembalo
Genre: Keyboard Sonatas
Source description
Original title: Sonata Undecima.
Material: Manuscript, Autograph, 1 parts: 5f.

Incipits (D-MÜs/ SANT Hs 3389)

1.1.1 cemb, c Andantino; G minor

1.2.1 cemb, 3/4 Andante; G minor

1.3.1 cemb, 3/4 Allegro; G minor

Incipit: (I-MC/ 6-A-1/15b)

Library: a) Santini-Sammlung, Diözesanbibliothek, Münster
b) Monumento Nazionale di Montecassino, Biblioteca

Siglum/ signature: D-MÜs/ SANT Hs 3389 (Nr. 11)
I-MC/ 6-A-1/15b

Notes:
Opening bar of I-MC/ 6-A-1/15b differing rhythmic structure (see Incipit).
Third movement missing from I-MC/ 6-A-1/15b

Title Page of collection: *Sonate per Cembalo di Ant° Reggio / Opera Prima / [left at head:] Originale*

Sonata in E major

Catalogue No: Hr 58
Key: E major
Scoring: cembalo
Genre: Keyboard Sonatas

Source description
Original title: Sonata Duodecima.
Material: Manuscript, Autograph, 1 parts: 5f.

Incipits

1.1.1 3/4 Andante; E major

1.2.1 c Andantino; E minor
1.3.1 3/4 Andante; E major
1.4.1 3/8 Presto; E major
1.5.1 3/4 Larghetto; E major
1.6.1 3/8 Minué.; E major

Library: a) Santini-Sammlung, Diözesanbibliothek, Münster
b) Monumento Nazionale di Montecassino, Biblioteca
Siglum/ signature: D-MÜs/ SANT Hs 3389 (Nr. 12)
I-MC/ 6-A-1/15c
Notes:

Literature: *The Breitkopf Thematic Catalogue. The six parts and sixteen supplements 1762-1787*, suppl.7: 1772, clm.473 (New York, 1966)
"*IV Sonate di Antonio Reggio, a cembalo Solo Amsterd.*" (I)

a) Title Page of collection: *Sonate per Cembalo di Ant° Reggio / Opera Prima / [left at head:] Originale*
b) In I-MC/ 6-A-1/15c movements vary : 1.2.1 c Presto; E minor; 1.3.1 3/4 Andante; E major; 1.4.1 3/8 Minuè; E major

Sonata in F major

Catalogue No:	Hr 59
Date:	[n.d.]
Key:	F major
Scoring:	cembalo
Genre:	Keyboard Sonatas

Source description

Original title:	Sonata Prima.
Material:	Manuscript, Autograph, 1 parts: 4f.

Incipits

1.1.1 3/4 Andantino; F major

1.2.1 c Allegro con spirito; F major

Library:	Santini-Sammlung, Diözesanbibliothek, Münster
Siglum/ signature:	D-MÜs/ SANT Hs 3390 (Nr. 1)

Notes:
Title page of collection: *Sonate per Cembalo di Ant° Reggio / Opera Seconda / [left at head:] Originale*

Sonata in B minor

Catalogue No:	Hr 60
Date:	[n.d.]
Key:	B minor
Scoring:	cembalo
Genre:	Keyboard Sonatas

Source description

Original title:	Sonata Seconda.
Material:	Manuscript, Autograph 1 parts: 4f

Incipits

1.1.1 c Andante assai; B minor

1.2.1 3/4 Allegro non presto; B minor

Library:	Santini-Sammlung, Diözesanbibliothek, Münster
Siglum/ signature:	D-MÜs/ SANT Hs 3390 (Nr. 2)

Notes

Title page of collection: *Sonate per Cembalo di Ant° Reggio / Opera Seconda / [left at head:] Originale*

Sonata in C major

Catalogue No:	Hr 61
Date:	[n.d.]
Key:	C major
Scoring:	cembalo
Genre:	Keyboard Sonatas

Source description

Original title:	Sonata Terza.
Material:	Manuscript, Autograph, 1 parts: 4f

Incipits

1.1.1 cemb, 3/8 Andante assai; C major

1.2.1 cemb, 3/4 Tempo di minuè; C major

Library:	Santini-Sammlung, Diözesanbibliothek, Münster
Siglum/ signature:	D-MÜs/ SANT Hs 3390 (Nr. 3)

Notes:
Title page of collection: *Sonate per Cembalo di Ant° Reggio / Opera Seconda / [left at head:] Originale*

Sonata in B♭ minor

Catalogue No:	Hr 62
Date:	[n.d.]
Key:	B♭ minor
Scoring:	cembalo
Genre:	Keyboard Sonatas

Source description

Original title:	Sonata Quarta.
Material:	Manuscript, Autograph, 1 parts: 4f.

Incipits

1.1.1 cemb, 2/4 Andantino; B♭ minor

1.2.1 cemb, 3/8 Presto; B♭ minor

Library:	Santini-Sammlung, Diözesanbibliothek, Münster
Siglum/ signature:	D-MÜs/ SANT Hs 3390 (Nr. 4)

Notes:
Title page of collection: *Sonate per Cembalo di Ant° Reggio / Opera Seconda / [left at head:] Originale*

Sonata in A major

Catalogue No:	Hr 63
Date:	[n.d.]
Key:	A major
Scoring:	cembalo
Genre:	Keyboard Sonatas

Source description

Original title:	Sonata Quinta.
Material:	Manuscript, Autograph, 1 parts: 4f.

Incipits

1.1.1 cemb, c Allegro; A major

1.2.1 cemb, 3/8 Tempo di minuè; A major

Library:	Santini-Sammlung, Diözesanbibliothek, Münster
Siglum/ signature:	D-MÜs/ SANT Hs 3390 (Nr. 5)

Notes:
Title page of collection: *Sonate per Cembalo di Ant° Reggio / Opera Seconda / [left at head:] Originale*

Sonata in G major

Catalogue No:	Hr 64
Date:	[n.d.]
Key:	G major
Scoring:	cembalo
Genre:	Keyboard Sonatas

Source description

Original title:	Sonata Sesta.
Material:	Manuscript, Autograph, 1 parts: 4f.

Incipits

1.1.1 cemb, 2/4 Allegro moderato; G major

1.2.1 cemb, 12/8 Presto; G major

Library:	Santini-Sammlung, Diözesanbibliothek, Münster
Siglum/ signature:	D-MÜs/ SANT Hs 3390 (Nr. 6)

Notes;
Title page of collection: *Sonate per Cembalo di Ant° Reggio / Opera Seconda / [left at head:] Originale*

Sonata in D minor

Catalogue No:	Hr 65
Date:	[n.d.]
Key:	D minor
Scoring:	cembalo
Genre:	Keyboard Sonatas

Source description

Original title:	Sonata Settima.
Material:	Manuscript, Autograph, 1 parts: 7f.

Incipits

1.1.1 cemb, c Allegro; D minor

1.2.1 cemb, 3/8 Minué.; D minor

Library:	Santini-Sammlung, Diözesanbibliothek, Münster
Siglum/ signature:	D-MÜs/ SANT Hs 3390 (Nr. 7)

Notes:
Title page of collection: *Sonate per Cembalo di Ant° Reggio / Opera Seconda / [left at head:] Originale*

Sonata in E major

Catalogue No:	Hr 66
Date:	[n.d.]
Key:	E major
Scoring:	cembalo
Genre:	Keyboard Sonatas

Source description

Original title:	Sonata Ottava.
Material:	Manuscript, Autograph, 1 parts: 4f.

Incipits

1.1.1 cemb, 3/4 Andantino; E major

1.2.1 cemb, c Allegro e con spirito; E major

Library;	Santini-Sammlung, Diözesanbibliothek, Münster
Siglum/ signature:	D-MÜs/ SANT Hs 3390 (Nr. 8)

Notes:
Title page of collection: *Sonate per Cembalo di Ant° Reggio / Opera Seconda / [left at head:] Originale*

Sonata in A♭ major

Catalogue No:	Hr 67
Date:	[n.d.]
Key:	A♭ major
Scoring:	cembalo
Genre:	Keyboard Sonatas

Source description

Original title:	Sonata Nona.
Material:	Manuscript, Autograph, 1 parts: 4f.

Incipits

1.1.1 cemb, 2/4 Allegro non presto; A♭ major

1.2.1 cemb, 3/8 Tempo di minuè; A♭ major

Library:	Santini-Sammlung, Diözesanbibliothek, Münster
Siglum/ signature:	D-MÜs/ SANT Hs 3390 (Nr. 9)

Notes:
Title page of collection: *Sonate per Cembalo di Ant° Reggio / Opera Seconda / [left at head:] Originale*

Sonata in F minor

Catalogue No:	Hr 68
Date:	[n.d.]
Key:	F minor
Scoring:	cembalo
Genre:	Keyboard Sonatas

Source description

Original title:	Sonata Decima.
Material:	Manuscript, Autograph, 1 parts: 5f.

Incipits

1.1.1 cemb, 3/4 Allegro non presto; F minor

1.2.1 cemb, c Allegro; F minor

Library:	Santini-Sammlung, Diözesanbibliothek, Münster
Siglum/ signature:	D-MÜs/ SANT Hs 3390 (Nr. 10)

Notes:
Title page of collection: *Sonate per Cembalo di Ant° Reggio / Opera Seconda / [left at head:] Originale*

Sonata in D major

Catalogue No: Hr 69
Date: [n.d.]
Key: D major
Scoring: cembalo
Genre: Keyboard Sonatas
Source description
Original title: Sonata Undecima.
Material: Manuscript, Autograph, 1 parts: 4f.
Incipits

1.1.1 cemb, c Allegro non presto; D major

1.2.1 cemb, 3/4 Allegretto; D major

Library: Santini-Sammlung, Diözesanbibliothek, Münster

Siglum/ signature: D-MÜs/ SANT Hs 3390 (Nr. 11)

Notes;
Title page of collection: *Sonate per Cembalo di Ant° Reggio / Opera Seconda / [left at head:] Originale*

Sonata in B♭ major

Catalogue No:	Hr 70
Date:	[n.d.]
Key:	B♭ major
Scoring:	cembalo
Genre:	Keyboard Sonatas

Source description

Original title:	Sonata Duodecima.
Material:	Manuscript, Autograph, 1 parts: 4f.

Incipits

1.1.1 cemb, 12/8 Un poco allegro; B♭ major

1.2.1 cemb, 2/4 Allegro assai; B♭ major

Library:	Santini-Sammlung, Diözesanbibliothek, Münster
Siglum/ signature:	D-MÜs/ SANT Hs 3390 (Nr. 12)

Notes:
Title page of collection: *Sonate per Cembalo di Ant° Reggio / Opera Seconda / [left at head:] Originale*

Sonata in B♭ major

Catalogue No:	Hr 71
Date:	[n.d.]
Key:	B♭ major
Scoring:	cembalo
Genre:	Keyboard Sonatas

Source description

Original title:	Sonata Prima.
Material:	Manuscript, Autograph, 1 parts: 4f

Incipits

1.1.1 cemb, 6/8 Andante assai; B♭ major

1.2.1 cemb, 3/8 Presto; B♭ major

Library:	Santini-Sammlung, Diözesanbibliothek, Münster
Siglum/ signature:	D-MÜs/ SANT Hs 3391 (Nr. 1)

Notes:
Title page of collection: *Sonate per Cembalo di Ant° Reggio / Opera Terza / [left at head:] Originale*

Sonata in E minor

Catalogue No:	Hr 72
Date:	[n.d.]
Key:	E minor
Scoring:	cembalo
Genre:	Keyboard Sonatas

Source description

Original title:	Sonata Seconda.
Material:	Manuscript, Autograph, 1 parts: 4f.

Incipits

1.1.1 cemb, 3/4 Un poco andante; E minor

1.2.1 cemb, 3/4 Prestissimo; E minor

Library:	Santini-Sammlung, Diözesanbibliothek, Münster
Siglum/ signature:	D-MÜs/ SANT Hs 3391 (Nr. 2)

Notes:
Title page of collection: *Sonate per Cembalo di Ant° Reggio / Opera Terza / [left at head:] Originale*

Sonata in B major

Catalogue No:	Hr 73
Date:	[n.d.]
Key:	B major
Scoring:	cembalo
Genre:	Keyboard Sonatas

Source description

Original title:	Sonata Terza.
Material:	Manuscript, Autograph, 1 parts: 5f.

Incipits

1.1.1 cemb, 3/4 Andante; B major

1.2.1 cemb, 3/8 Presto; B major

Library:	Santini-Sammlung, Diözesanbibliothek, Münster
Siglum/ signature:	D-MÜs/ SANT Hs 3391 (Nr. 3)

Notes:
Title page of collection: *Sonate per Cembalo di Ant° Reggio / Opera Terza / [left at head:] Originale*

Sonata in C major

Catalogue No:	Hr 74
Date:	[n.d.]
Key:	C major
Scoring :	cembalo
Genre:	Keyboard Sonatas

Source description

Original title:	Sonata Quarta.
Material:	Manuscript, Autograph, 1 parts: 4f.

Incipits

1.1.1 cemb, 3/4 Adagio; C major

1.2.1 cemb, 3/8 Presto; C major

Library:	Santini-Sammlung, Diözesanbibliothek, Münster
Siglum/ signature:	D-MÜs/ SANT Hs 3391 (Nr. 4)

Notes:
Title page of collection: *Sonate per Cembalo di Ant° Reggio / Opera Terza / [left at head:] Originale*

Sonata in E♭ major

Catalogue No:	Hr 75
Date:	[n.d.]
Key:	E♭ major
Scoring:	cembalo
Genre:	Keyboard Sonatas
Source description	
Original title:	Sonata Quinta.
Material:	Manuscript, Autograph, 1 parts: 4f.

Incipits

1.1.1 cemb, 3/4 Andantino; E♭ major

1.2.1 cemb, c Allegro; E♭ major

Library:	Santini-Sammlung, Diözesanbibliothek, Münster
Siglum/ signature:	D-MÜs/ SANT Hs 3391 (Nr. 5)

Notes:
Title page of collection: *Sonate per Cembalo di Ant° Reggio / Opera Terza / [left at head:] Originale*

Sonata in E♭ major

Catalogue No: Hr 76
Date: [n.d.]
Key: E♭ major
Scoring: cembalo
Genre: Keyboard Sonatas
Source description
Original title: Sonato Sesta
Material: Manuscript, Autograph,1 parts: 2f.
Incipits
1.1.1, 2/4 Presto; E♭ major

1.2.1, 3/4 Minué.; E♭ major

Library: Santini-Sammlung, Diözesanbibliothek, Münster

Siglum/ signature: D-MÜs/ SANT Hs 3388 (Nr. 6)

Notes
Title page of collection: *Sonate per Cembalo di Ant° Reggio / Opera Terza / [left at head:] Originale*

Sonata in D major

Catalogue No:	Hr 77
Date:	[n.d.]
Key:	D major
Scoring:	cembalo
Genre:	Keyboard Sonatas

Source description

Original title:	Sonata Settima.
Material:	Manuscript, Autograph, 1 parts: 4f.

Incipits

1.1.1 c Andante; D major

1.2.1 3/4 Tempo di minuè con spirito; D major

Library:	Santini-Sammlung, Diözesanbibliothek, Münster
Siglum/ signature:	D-MÜs/ SANT Hs 3391 (Nr. 7)

Notes:
Title page of collection: *Sonate per Cembalo di Ant° Reggio / Opera Terza / [left at head:] Originale*

Sonata in E♭ minor

Catalogue No:	Hr 78
Date:	[n.d.]
Key:	E♭ minor
Scoring:	cembalo
Genre:	Keyboard Sonatas

Source description

Original title:	Sonata Ottava.
Material:	Manuscript, Autograph, 1 parts: 4f.

Incipits

1.1.1 cemb, c/ Andantino; E♭ minor

1.2.1 cemb, 3/8 Allegro; E♭ minor

Library:	Santini-Sammlung, Diözesanbibliothek, Münster
Siglum/ signature:	D-MÜs/ SANT Hs 3391 (Nr. 8)

Notes:
Title page of collection: *Sonate per Cembalo di Ant° Reggio / Opera Terza / [left at head:] Originale*

Sonata in G major

Catalogue No: Hr 79
Date: [n.d.]
Key: G major
Scoring: cembalo
Genre: Keyboard Sonatas
Source description
Original title: Sonata Nona.
Material: Manuscript, Autograph, 1 parts: 4f.
Incipits

1.1.1 cemb, c Allegro con brio; G major

1.2.1 cemb, 3/8 Allegro; G major

Library: Santini-Sammlung, Diözesanbibliothek, Münster

Siglum/ signature: D-MÜs/ SANT Hs 3391 (Nr. 9)

Notes:
Title page of collection: *Sonate per Cembalo di Ant° Reggio / Opera Terza / [left at head:] Originale*

Sonata in F major

Catalogue No:	Hr 80
Date:	[n.d.]
Key:	F major
Scoring:	cembalo
Genre:	Keyboard Sonatas

Source description

Original title:	Sonata Decima.
Material:	Manuscript. Autograph, 1 parts: 5f.

Incipits

1.1.1 3/4 Andante un poco; F major

1.2. c Allegro assai; F major

Library;	Santini-Sammlung, Diözesanbibliothek, Münster
Siglum/ signature:	D-MÜs/ SANT Hs 3391 (Nr. 10)

Notes;
Title page of collection: *Sonate per Cembalo di Ant° Reggio / Opera Terza / [left at head:] Originale*

Sonata in C minor

Catalogue No:	Hr 81
Date:	[n.d.]
Key:	C minor
Scoring:	cembalo
Genre:	Keyboard Sonatas

Source description

Original title:	Sonata Undecima.
Material:	Manuscript, Autograph, 1 parts: 4f.

Incipits

1.1.1 cemb, c/ Andantino; C minor

1.2.1 cemb, 3/8 Presto; C minor

Library;	Santini-Sammlung, Diözesanbibliothek, Münster
Siglum/ signature:	D-MÜs/ SANT Hs 3391 (Nr. 11)

Notes:
Title page of collection: *Sonate per Cembalo di Ant° Reggio / Opera Terza / [left at head:] Originale*

Sonata in A major

Catalogue No:	Hr 82
Date:	[n.d.]
Key:	A major
Scoring:	cembalo
Genre:	Keyboard Sonatas

Source description

Original title:	Sonata Duodecima.
Material:	Manuscripts, Autograph, 1 parts: 4f.

Incipits

1.1.1 cemb, c; 6/8 Presto assai; A major

1.2.1 cemb, 2/4 Allegro moderato; A major

Library:	Santini-Sammlung, Diözesanbibliothek, Münster
Siglum/ signature:	D-MÜs/ SANT Hs 3391 (Nr. 12)

Notes:
Title page of collection: *Sonate per Cembalo di Ant° Reggio / Opera Terza / [left at head:] Originale*

Sonata in F major

Catalogue No:	Hr 83
Date:	[n.d.]
Key:	F major
Scoring:	cembalo
Genre:	Keyboard Sonatas

Source description

Original title:	I. | Sonata per Cembalo | Opera Quarta | Originale di Antº Reggio
Material:	Manuscript, Autograph, 1 parts: 5f.

Incipits

1.1.1 cemb, 3/4 Andantino; F major

1.2.1 cemb, 2/4 Allegretto; F major

1.3.1 cemb, 6/8 Presto; F major

Library:	Santini-Sammlung, Diözesanbibliothek, Münster
Siglum/ signature:	D-MÜs/ SANT Hs 3387 (Nr. 1)
Notes:	

Sonata in A major

Catalogue No:	Hr 84
Date:	[n.d.]
Key:	A major
Scoring:	cembalo
Genre:	Keyboard Sonatas

Source description

Original title:	III | Sonata per Cembalo
Material:	Manuscript, Autograph, 1 parts: 5f.

Incipits

1.1.1 cemb, 3/4 Adagio; A major

1.2.1 cemb, 2/4 Presto; A major

1.3.1 cemb, c/ Allegro assai; A major

Library:	Santini-Sammlung, Diözesanbibliothek, Münster
Siglum/ signature:	D-MÜs/ SANT Hs 3387 (Nr. 2)
Notes:	

Sonata in E major

Catalogue No:	Hr 85
Date:	[n.d.]
Key:	E major
Scoring:	cembalo
Genre:	Keyboard Sonatas

Source description

Original title:	IV	Sonata per Cembalo.
Material:	Manuscript, Autograph, 1 parts: 4f.

Incipits

1.1.1 cemb, 3/4 Un poco larghetto; E major

1.2.1 cemb, c Vivace assai; E major

1.3.1 cemb, 3/8 Presto; E major

Library:	Santini-Sammlung, Diözesanbibliothek, Münster
Siglum/ signature:	D-MÜs/ SANT Hs 3387 (Nr. 3)
Notes:	

Sonata in B♭ major

Catalogue No:	Hr 86
Date:	[n.d.]
Key;	B♭ major
Scoring:	cembalo
Genre:	Keyboard Sonatas

Source description

Original title:	V | Sonata per Cembalo.
Material:	Manuscript, Autograph, 1 parts: 4f.

Incipits

1.1.1 cemb, c Andante; B♭ major

1.2.1 cemb, 3/8 Lento; B♭ major

1.3.1 cemb, 6/8 Allegro assai; B♭ major

Library:	Santini-Sammlung, Diözesanbibliothek, Münster
Siglum/ signature:	D-MÜs/ SANT Hs 3387 (Nr. 4)
Notes:	

Sonata in C minor

Catalogue No:	Hr 87
Date:	[n.d.]
Key:	C minor
Scoring:	cembalo
Genre:	Keyboard Sonatas

Source description

Original title:	VI	Sonata per Cembalo.
Material:	Manuscript, Autograph, 1 parts: 4f.

Incipits

1.1.1 cemb, 3/4 Andantino; C minor

1.2.1 cemb, c Allegro non molto; C minor

1.3.1 cemb, c/ Allegro assai; C minor

Library:	Santini-Sammlung, Diözesanbibliothek, Münster
Siglum/ signature:	D-MÜs/ SANT Hs 3387 (Nr. 5)
Notes :	

Sonata in C major

Catalogue No: Hr 88
Date: [n.d.]
Key: C major
Scoring: cembalo
Genre: Keyboard Sonatas

Source description

Original title: VII | Sonata per Cembalo.
Material: Manuscript, Autograph, 1 parts: 4f.

Incipits

1.1.1 cemb, 3/4 Larghetto; C major

1.2.1 cemb, c Allegro moderato; C major

1.3.1 cemb, 12/8 Pastorale. Andante; C major

Library; Santini-Sammlung, Diözesanbibliothek, Münster

Siglum/ signature: D-MÜs/ SANT Hs 3387 (Nr. 6)

Notes

Sonata in D major

Catalogue No: Hr 89
Date: [n.d.]
Key: D major
Scoring: cembalo
Genre: Keyboard Sonatas
Source description
Original title: VIII | Sonata per Cembalo.
Material: Manuscript, Autograph, 1 parts: 4f.
Incipits

1.1.1 cemb, c Andantino; D major

1.2.1 cemb, 2/4 Presto; D major

1.3.1 cemb, 3/8 Allegretto; D major

Library: Santini-Sammlung, Diözesanbibliothek, Münster

Siglum/ signature: D-MÜs/ SANT Hs 3387 (Nr. 7)
Notes:

Sonata in F# minor

Catalogue No:	Hr 90
Date:	[n.d.]
Key:	F# minor
Scoring:	cembalo
Genre:	Keyboard Sonatas

Source description

Original title:	IX | Sonata per Cembalo.
Material:	Manuscript, Autograph, 1 parts: 5f.

Incipits

1.1.1 cemb, c/ Larghetto; F# minor

1.2.1 cemb, 2/4 Presto; F# minor

1.3.1 cemb, 3/8 Allegretto; F# minor

Library:	Santini-Sammlung, Diözesanbibliothek, Münster
Siglum/ signature:	D-MÜs/ SANT Hs 3387 (Nr. 8)
Notes:	

Sonata in G major

Catalogue No:	Hr 91
Date:	[n.d.]
Key:	G major
Scoring:	cembalo
Genre:	Keyboard Sonatas

Source description

Original title:	X | Sonata per Cembalo.
Material:	Manuscript, Autograph, 1 parts: 4f.

Incipits

1.1.1 cemb, c Andante; G major

1.2.1 cemb, 3/4 Allegro; G major

1.3.1 cemb, 3/8 Andante; G major

Library:	Santini-Sammlung, Diözesanbibliothek, Münster
Siglum/ signature:	D-MÜs/ SANT Hs 3387 (Nr. 9)
Notes:	

Sonata in A♭ minor

Catalogue No:	Hr 92
Date:	[n.d.]
Key:	Ab minor
Scoring:	cembalo
Genre:	Keyboard Sonatas

Source description

Original title:	XI | Sonata per Cembalo.
Material:	Manuscript, Autograph, 1 parts: 4f.

Incipits

1.1.1 cemb, 2/4 Andante staccato; A♭ minor

1.2.1 cemb, 3/4 Allegro; A♭ minor

1.3.1 cemb, 2/4 Presto; A♭minor

Library:	Santini-Sammlung, Diözesanbibliothek, Münster
Siglum/ signature:	D-MÜs/ SANT Hs 3387 (Nr. 10)
Notes:	

Sonata in F# major

Catalogue No:	Hr 93
Date:	[n.d.]
Key:	F# major
Scoring:	cembalo
Genre:	Keyboard Sonatas

Source description

Original title:	XII	Sonata per Cembalo.
Material:	Manuscript, Autograph, 1 parts: 4f.

Incipits

1.1.1 cemb, c Andante; F# major

1.2.1 cemb, 3/4 Allegro; F# major

1.3.1 cemb, 2/4 Presto; F# major

Library:	Santini-Sammlung, Diözesanbibliothek, Münster
Siglum/ signature:	D-MÜs/ SANT Hs 3387 (Nr. 11)
Notes:	

Sonata in C minor

Catalogue No:	Hr 94
Date:	1774
Key:	C minor
Scoring:	cembalo
Genre:	Keyboard Sonatas

Source description

Original title:	I.
Material:	Manuscript, Autograph, 1 parts: 2f.

Incipits

1.1.1 cemb, 3/4 Andante; C minor

1.2.1 cemb, 3/8 Minué.; C minor

Library:	Santini-Sammlung, Diözesanbibliothek, Münster
Siglum/ signature:	D-MÜs/ SANT Hs 3388 (Nr. 1)

Notes:
Title page of collection: *Sonatine per Cembalo / [at head:] Opera Quinta di XXIV. Sonatine A[nno] 1774 Originale di Ant° Reggio*

Sonata in G major

Catalogue No:	Hr 95
Date:	1774
Key:	G major
Scoring:	cembalo
Genre:	Keyboard Sonatas

Source description

Original title:	II.
Material:	Manuscript, Autograph, 1 parts: 1f.

Incipits

1.1.1 cemb, 6/8 Andantino; G major

1.2.1 cemb, 3/4 Minué.; G major

Library:	Santini-Sammlung, Diözesanbibliothek, Münster
Siglum/ signature:	D-MÜs/ SANT Hs 3388 (Nr. 2)

Notes:
Title page of collection: *Sonatine per Cembalo / [at head:] Opera Quinta di XXIV. Sonatine A[nno] 1774 Originale di Ant° Reggio*

Sonata in F major

Catalogue No:	Hr 96
Date:	1774
Key;	F major
Scoring :	cembalo
Genre:	Keyboard Sonatas

Source description

Original title:	III.
Material:	Manuscript, Autograph, 1 parts: 1f.

Incipits

1.1.1 cemb, c Allegro assai; F major

1.2.1 cemb, 3/4 Tempo di minuè; G major

Library;	Santini-Sammlung, Diözesanbibliothek, Münster
Siglum/ signature:	D-MÜs/ SANT Hs 3388 (Nr. 3)

Notes:
Title page of collection: *Sonatine per Cembalo / [at head:] Opera Quinta di XXIV. Sonatine A[nno] 1774 Originale di Ant° Reggio*

Sonata in B♭ major

Catalogue No:	Hr 97
Date:	1774
Key:	B♭ major
Scoring:	cembalo
Genre:	Keyboard Sonatas
Source description	
Original title:	IV.
Material:	Manuscript, Autograph, 1 parts: 1f.

Incipits

1.1.1 cemb, 3/4 Andantino espressivo; B♭ major

1.2.1 cemb, 3/4 Minué.; B♭ major

Library:	Santini-Sammlung, Diözesanbibliothek, Münster
Siglum/ signature:	D-MÜs/ SANT Hs 3388 (Nr. 4)

Notes;
Title page of collection: *Sonatine per Cembalo / [at head:] Opera Quinta di XXIV. Sonatine A[nno] 1774 Originale di Ant° Reggio*

Sonata in A major

Catalogue No:	Hr 98
Date:	1774
Key:	A major
Scoring:	cembalo
Genre:	Keyboard Sonatas

Source description

Original title:	V.
Material:	Manuscript, Autograph, 1 parts: 2f.

Incipits

1.1.1 cemb, 3/4 Andante; A major

1.2.1 cemb, 3/8 A tempo di minué; A major

Library:	Santini-Sammlung, Diözesanbibliothek, Münster
Siglum/ signature:	D-MÜs/ SANT Hs 3388 (Nr. 5)

Notes:
Title page of collection: *Sonatine per Cembalo / [at head:] Opera Quinta di XXIV. Sonatine A[nno] 1774 Originale di Ant° Reggio*

Sonata in E♭ major

Catalogue No:	Hr 99
Date:	1774
Key:	E♭ major
Scoring:	cembalo
Genre:	Keyboard Sonatas

Source description

Original title:	VI.
Material:	Manuscript, Autograph,1 parts: 2f.

Incipits

1.1.1, 2/4 Presto; E♭ major

1.2.1, 3/4 Minué.; E♭ major

Library:	Santini-Sammlung, Diözesanbibliothek, Münster
Siglum/ signature:	D-MÜs/ SANT Hs 3388 (Nr. 6)

Notes:
Title page of collection: *Sonatine per Cembalo / [at head:] Opera Quinta di XXIV. Sonatine A[nno] 1774 Originale di Ant° Reggio*

Sonata in G minor

Catalogue No:	Hr 100
Date:	1774
Key:	G minor
Scoring :	cembalo
Genre:	Keyboard Sonatas

Source description

Original title:	VII.
Material:	Manuscript, Autograph, 1 parts: 2f.

Incipits

1.1.1 cemb, c Allegro; G minor

1.2.1 cemb, 3/4 Minué.; G minor

Library:	Santini-Sammlung, Diözesanbibliothek, Münster
Siglum/ signature:	D-MÜs/ SANT Hs 3388 (Nr. 7)

Notes:
Title page of collection: *Sonatine per Cembalo / [at head:] Opera Quinta di XXIV. Sonatine A[nno] 1774 Originale di Ant° Reggio*

Sonata in C major

Catalogue No:	Hr 101
Date:	1774
Key:	C major
Scoring:	cembalo
Genre:	Keyboard Sonatas

Source description

Original title:	VIII.
Material:	Manuscript, Autograph, 1 parts: 2f.

Incipits

1.1.1 cemb, 6/8 Andantino; C major

1.2.1 cemb, 3/4 Minué.; C major

Library:	Santini-Sammlung, Diözesanbibliothek, Münster
Siglum/ signature:	D-MÜs/ SANT Hs 3388 (Nr. 8)

Notes:
Title page of collection: *Sonatine per Cembalo* / [at head:] *Opera Quinta di XXIV. Sonatine A[nno] 1774 Originale di Ant° Reggio*

Sonata in D minor

Catalogue No:	Hr 102
Date:	1774
Key:	D minor
Scoring:	cembalo
Genre:	Keyboard Sonatas

Source description

Original title:	IX.
Material:	Manuscript. Autograph, 1 parts: 2f.

Incipits

1.1.1 cemb, c Allegretto; D minor

1.2.1 cemb, 3/4 Minué.; D minor

Library:	Santini-Sammlung, Diözesanbibliothek, Münster
Siglum/ signature:	D-MÜs/ SANT Hs 3388 (Nr. 9)

Notes:
Title page of collection: *Sonatine per Cembalo / [at head:] Opera Quinta di XXIV. Sonatine A[nno] 1774 Originale di Ant° Reggio*

Sonata in C major

Catalogue No: Hr 103
Date: 1774
Key: C major
Scoring: cembalo
Genre: Keyboard Sonatas
Source description
Original title: X.
Material: Manuscript, Autograph, 1 parts: 2f.

Incipits

1.1.1 cemb, c Allegretto; C major

1.2.1 cemb, 3/4 Minué.; C major

Library: Santini-Sammlung, Diözesanbibliothek, Münster

Siglum/ signature: D-MÜs/ SANT Hs 3388 (Nr. 10)

Notes:
Title page of collection: *Sonatine per Cembalo* / *[at head:] Opera Quinta di XXIV. Sonatine A[nno] 1774 Originale di Ant° Reggio*

Sonata in D major

Catalogue No:	Hr 104
Date:	1774
Key:	D major
Scoring:	cembalo
Genre:	Keyboard Sonatas

Source description

Original title:	XI.
Material:	Manuscript, Autograph, 1 parts: 3f.

Incipits

1.1.1 cemb, 3/4 Andante; D major

1.2.1 cemb, 3/8 Presto; D major

Library:	Santini-Sammlung, Diözesanbibliothek, Münster
Siglum/ signature:	D-MÜs/ SANT Hs 3388 (Nr. 11)

Notes:
Title page of collection: *Sonatine per Cembalo / [at head:] Opera Quinta di XXIV. Sonatine A[nno] 1774 Originale di Ant° Reggio*

Sonata in B♭ major

Catalogue No:	Hr 105
Date:	1774
Key:	B♭ major
Scoring:	cembalo
Genre:	Keyboard Sonatas

Source description

Original title:	XII.
Material:	Manuscript, Autograph, 1 parts: 3f.

Incipits

1.1.1 cemb, c Andantino; B♭ major

1.2.1 cemb, 3/8 Presto; B♭ major

Library:	Santini-Sammlung, Diözesanbibliothek, Münster
Siglum/ signature:	D-MÜs/ SANT Hs 3388 (Nr. 12)

Notes:
Title page of collection: *Sonatine per Cembalo / [at head:] Opera Quinta di XXIV. Sonatine A[nno] 1774 Originale di Ant° Reggio*

Sonata in B♭ major

Catalogue No:	Hr 106
Date:	1774
Key;	B♭ major
Scoring:	cembalo
Genre:	Keyboard Sonatas

Source description

Original title:	XIII.
Material:	Manuscript, Autograph, 1 parts: 3f.

Incipits

1.1.1, c Andantino; B♭ major

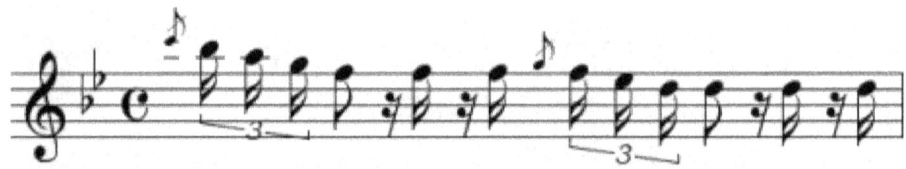

1.2.1 3/8 Presto; B♭ major

Library;	Santini-Sammlung, Diözesanbibliothek, Münster
Siglum/ signature:	D-MÜs/ SANT Hs 3388 (Nr. 13)

Notes:
Title page of collection: *Sonatine per Cembalo / [at head:] Opera Quinta di XXIV. Sonatine A[nno] 1774 Originale di Ant° Reggio*

Sonata in E♭ major

Catalogue No: Hr 107
Date: 1774
Key; E♭ major
Scoring: cembalo
Genre: Keyboard Sonatas
Source description
Original title: XIV.
Material: Manuscript, Autograph, 1 parts: 3f.
Incipits
1.1.1 cemb, 3/4 Grave; E♭ major

1.2.1 cemb, 3/8 Presto; E♭ major

Library: Santini-Sammlung, Diözesanbibliothek, Münster
Siglum/ signature: D-MÜs/ SANT Hs 3388 (Nr. 14)
Notes:
Title page of collection: *Sonatine per Cembalo* / *[at head:] Opera Quinta di XXIV. Sonatine A[nno] 1774 Originale di Ant° Reggio*

Sonata in F major

Catalogue No:	Hr 108
Date:	1774
Key:	F major
Scoring:	cembalo
Genre:	Keyboard Sonatas

Source description

Original title:	XV.
Material:	Manuscript, Autograph, 1 parts: 2f.

Incipits

1.1.1 cemb, 3/4 Andante; F major

1.2.1 cemb, 3/4 Allegro; F major

Library:	Santini-Sammlung, Diözesanbibliothek, Münster
Siglum/ signature:	D-MÜs/ SANT Hs 3388 (Nr. 15)

Notes:
Title page of collection: *Sonatine per Cembalo / [at head:] Opera Quinta di XXIV. Sonatine A[nno] 1774 Originale di Ant° Reggio*

Sonata in D Major

Catalogue No:	Hr 109
Date:	1774
Key:	D Major
Scoring:	Cembalo
Genre:	Keyboard Sonatas

Source Description

Original title :	XVI.
Material :	Manuscript, Autograph, 1 parts: 1f.

Incipits

1.1.1 c / Larghetto, D major

1.2.1 3/8 Presto assai, D major

Library:	Santini-Sammlung, Diözesanbibliothek, Münster
Siglum/ signature:	D-MÜs / SANT Hs 3388 (No. 16)

Notes:
Title page of collection: *Sonatine per Cembalo* / *[at head:] Opera Quinta di XXIV. Sonatine A[nno] 1774 Originale di Ant° Reggio*

Sonata in Eb major

Catalogue No:	Hr 110
Date:	1774
Key:	Eb major
Scoring:	cembalo
Genre:	Keyboard Sonatas

Source description

Original title:	XVII.
Material:	Manuscript, Autograph, 1 parts: 2f.

Incipits

1.1.1 cemb, 3/4 Andantino; Eb major

1.2.1 cemb, 2/4 Allegro; Eb major

Library:	Santini-Sammlung, Diözesanbibliothek, Münster
Siglum/ signature:	D-MÜs/ SANT Hs 3388 (Nr. 17)

Notes:
Title page of collection: *Sonatine per Cembalo / [at head:] Opera Quinta di XXIV. Sonatine A[nno] 1774 Originale di Ant° Reggio*

Sonata in G major

Catalogue No:	Hr 111
Date:	1774
Key:	G major
Scoring:	cembalo
Genre:	Keyboard Sonatas

Source description

Original title:	XVIII.
Material:	Manuscript, Autograph, 1 parts: 3f.

Incipits

1.1.1 cemb, 2/4 Allegro; G major

1.2.1 cemb, 3/4 Minué. Moderato; G major

Library:	Santini-Sammlung, Diözesanbibliothek, Münster
Siglum/ signature:	D-MÜs/ SANT Hs 3388 (Nr. 18)

Notes:
Title page of collection: *Sonatine per Cembalo / [at head:] Opera Quinta di XXIV. Sonatine A[nno] 1774 Originale di Ant° Reggio*

Sonata in C major

Catalogue No:	Hr 112
Date:	1774
Key:	C major
Scoring:	cembalo
Genre:	Keyboard Sonatas

Source description

Original title:	XIX.
Material:	Manuscript, Autograph, 1 parts: 3f.

Incipits

1.1.1 cemb, 3/4 Andante; C major

1.2.1 cemb, 2/4 Non presto; C major

Library;	Santini-Sammlung, Diözesanbibliothek, Münster
Siglum/ signature:	D-MÜs/ SANT Hs 3388 (Nr. 19)

Notes:
Title page of collection: *Sonatine per Cembalo / [at head:] Opera Quinta di XXIV. Sonatine A[nno] 1774 Originale di Ant° Reggio*

Sonata in C minor

Catalogue No:	Hr 113
Date:	1774
Key:	C minor
Scoring:	cembalo
Genre:	Keyboard Sonatas

Source description

Original title:	XX.
Material:	Manuscript, Autograph, 1 parts: 3f.

Incipits

1.1.1 cemb, c Allegro; C minor

1.2.1 cemb, 2/4 Allegretto; C minor

Library:	Santini-Sammlung, Diözesanbibliothek, Münster
Siglum/ signature:	D-MÜs/ SANT Hs 3388 (Nr. 20)

Notes:
Title page of collection: *Sonatine per Cembalo* / [at head:] *Opera Quinta di XXIV. Sonatine A[nno] 1774 Originale di Ant° Reggio*

Sonata in A major

Catalogue No:	Hr 114
Date:	1774
Key:	A major
Scoring:	cembalo
Genre:	Keyboard Sonatas

Source description

Original title:	XXI.
Material:	Manuscript, Autograph, 1 parts: 3f.

Incipits

1.1.1 cemb, c Allegro; A major

1.2.1 cemb, 2/4 Prestissimo; A major

Library:	Santini-Sammlung, Diözesanbibliothek, Münster
Siglum/ signature:	D-MÜs/ SANT Hs 3388 (Nr. 21)

Notes:
Title page of collection: *Sonatine per Cembalo / [at head:] Opera Quinta di XXIV. Sonatine A[nno] 1774 Originale di Ant° Reggio*

Sonata in F minor

Catalogue No:	Hr 115
Date:	1774
Key:	F minor
Scoring:	cembalo
Genre:	Keyboard Sonatas

Source description

Original title:	XXII.
Material:	Manuscript, Autograph, 1 parts: 3f.

Incipits

1.1.1 cemb, 3/4 Andante assai; F minor

1.2.1 cemb, 2/4 Allegretto; F minor

Library:	Santini-Sammlung, Diözesanbibliothek, Münster
Siglum/ signature:	D-MÜs/ SANT Hs 3388 (Nr. 22)

Notes:
Title page of collection: *Sonatine per Cembalo / [at head:] Opera Quinta di XXIV. Sonatine A[nno] 1774 Originale di Antº Reggio*

Sonata in F major

Catalogue No:	Hr 116
Date:	1774
Key:	F major
Scoring:	cembalo
Genre:	Keyboard Sonatas

Source description

Original title:	XXIII.
Material:	Manuscript, Autograph, 1 parts: 3f

Incipits

1.1.1 cemb, c Allegro; F major

1.2.1 cemb, 3/4 Minué.; F major

Library:	Santini-Sammlung, Diözesanbibliothek, Münster
Siglum/ signature:	D-MÜs/ SANT Hs 3388 (Nr. 23)

Notes:
Title page of collection: *Sonatine per Cembalo / [at head:] Opera Quinta di XXIV. Sonatine A[nno] 1774 Originale di Ant° Reggio*

Sonata in E major

Catalogue No:	Hr 117
Date:	1774
Key:	E major
Scoring:	cembalo
Genre:	Keyboard Sonatas

Source description

Original title:	XXIV.
Material:	Manuscript, Autograph 1 parts: 3f

Incipits

1.1.1 c Allegro; E major

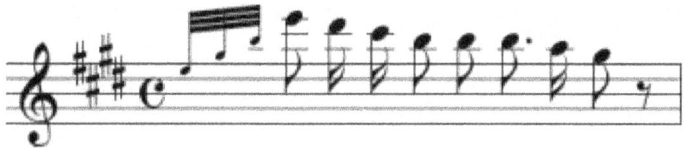

1.2.1 3/4 Minué.; E major

Library:	Santini-Sammlung, Diözesanbibliothek, Münster
Siglum/ signature:	D-MÜs/ SANT Hs 3388 (Nr. 24)

Notes
Title page of collection: *Sonatine per Cembalo / [at head:] Opera Quinta di XXIV. Sonatine A[nno] 1774 Originale di Ant° Reggio*

III Violoncello Sonatas

1. Index by Key

1. Index by Key:

C Major	Hr 129
C minor	Hr 118
D Major	Hr 125
D minor	Hr 123
E♭ Major	Hr 122 Hr 127
F Major	Hr 124
F minor	Hr 128
G Major	Hr 120
A Major	Hr 121
A minor	Hr 126
B♭ Major	Hr 119

Sonata in C minor

Catalogue No: Hr 118
Date: [n.d.]
Key: C minor
Scoring: violoncello (2)
Genre: Violoncello Sonatas
Source description
Original title: Sonatina a due Violoncelli.
Material: Manuscript, Autograph, score: 2f.
Incipits
1.1.1 violoncello 1, 3/4 Adagio; C minor

1.2.1 3/8 Allegro; C minor

Library: Santini-Sammlung, Diözesanbibliothek, Münster

Siglum/ signature: D-MÜs/ SANT Hs 3392 (Nr. 1)

Notes:
Title page of Collection: *Originale di Ant. Reggio. / Sonatine [a due Violoncelli e] di Liuto e Basso.*

Sonata in B♭ major

Catalogue No:	Hr 119
Date:	[n.d.]
Key:	B♭ major
Scoring:	violoncello (2)
Genre:	Violoncello Sonatas

Source description

Original title:	Sonatina a due Violoncelli.
Material:	Manuscript, Autograph, score: 2f.

Incipits

1.1.1 violoncello 1, c/ Andantino; B♭ major

1.2.1 3/8 Allegro; B♭ major

Library:	Santini-Sammlung, Diözesanbibliothek, Münster
Siglum/ signature:	D-MÜs/ SANT Hs 3392 (Nr. 2)

Notes:
Title page of Collection: *Originale di Ant. Reggio. / Sonatine [a due Violoncelli e] di Liuto e Basso.*

Sonata in G major

Catalogue No:	Hr 120
Date:	[n.d.]
Key:	G major
Scoring:	violoncello (2)
Genre:	Violoncello Sonatas

Source description

Original title:	Sonatina a due Violoncelli.
Material:	Manuscript, Autograph, score: 2f.

Incipits

1.1.1 violoncello 1, 2/4 Andantino; G major

1.2.1 3/4 Minué.; G major

Library:	Santini-Sammlung, Diözesanbibliothek, Münster
Siglum/ signature:	D-MÜs/ SANT Hs 3392 (Nr. 3)

Notes:
Title page of Collection: *Originale di Ant. Reggio. / Sonatine [a due Violoncelli e] di Liuto e Basso.*

Sonata in A major

Catalogue No:	Hr 121
Date:	[n.d.]
Key:	A major
Scoring:	violoncello (2)
Genre:	Violoncello Sonatas

Source description

Original title:	Sonatina a due Violoncelli.
Material:	Manuscript, Autograph, score: 2f.

Incipits

1.1.1 violoncello 1, 6/8 Andantino; A major

1.2.1 3/8 Allegro; A major

Library:	Santini-Sammlung, Diözesanbibliothek, Münster
Siglum/ signature:	D-MÜs/ SANT Hs 3392 (Nr. 4)

Notes:
Title page of Collection: *Originale di Ant. Reggio. / Sonatine [a due Violoncelli e] di Liuto e Basso.*

Sonata in E♭ major

Catalogue No:	Hr 122
Date:	[n.d.]
Key:	E♭ major
Scoring:	violoncello (2)
Genre:	Violoncello Sonatas

Source description

Original title:	Sonatina a due Violoncelli.
Material:	Manuscript, Autograph, score: 2f.

Incipits

1.1.1 violoncello 1, 3/4 Andante; E♭ major

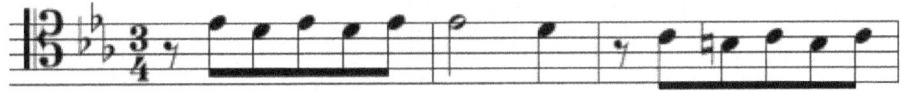

1.2.1 3/8 Allegro; E♭ major

Library:	Santini-Sammlung, Diözesanbibliothek, Münster
Siglum/ signature:	D-MÜs/ SANT Hs 3392 (Nr. 5)

Notes:
Title page of Collection: *Originale di Ant. Reggio. / Sonatine [a due Violoncelli e] di Liuto e Basso.*

Sonata in D minor

Catalogue No:	Hr 123
Date:	[n.d.]
Key:	D minor
Scoring:	violoncello (2)
Genre:	Violoncello Sonatas

Source description

Original title:	Sonatina a due Violoncelli.
Material:	Manuscript, Autograph, score: 2f.

Incipits

1.1.1 violoncello 1, c Andantino; D minor

1.2.1 3/4 Allegro; D minor

Library:	Santini-Sammlung, Diözesanbibliothek, Münster
Siglum/ signature:	D-MÜs/ SANT Hs 3392 (Nr. 6)

Notes:
Title page of Collection: *Originale di Ant. Reggio. / Sonatine [a due Violoncelli e] di Liuto e Basso.*

Sonata in F major

Catalogue No:	Hr 124
Date:	[n.d.]
Key:	F major
Scoring:	violoncello (2)
Genre:	Violoncello Sonatas

Source description

Original title:	Sonatina a due Violoncelli.
Material:	Manuscript, Autograph, score: 2f.

Incipits

1.1.1 violoncello 1, c Andante; F major

1.2.1 3/8 Minué.; F major

Library:	Santini-Sammlung, Diözesanbibliothek, Münster
Siglum/ signature:	D-MÜs/ SANT Hs 3392 (Nr. 7)

Notes:
Title page of Collection: *Originale di Ant. Reggio. / Sonatine [a due Violoncelli e] di Liuto e Basso.*

Sonata in D major

Catalogue No:	Hr 125
Date:	[n.d.]
Key:	D major
Scoring:	violoncello (2)
Genre:	Violoncello Sonatas

Source description

Original title:	Sonatina a due Violoncelli.
Material:	Manuscript, Autograph, score: 2f.

Incipits

1.1.1 violoncello 1, c Andante assai; D major

1.2.1 3/8 Presto assai; D major

Library:	Santini-Sammlung, Diözesanbibliothek, Münster
Siglum/ signature:	D-MÜs/ SANT Hs 3392 (Nr. 8)

Notes:
Title page of Collection: *Originale di Ant. Reggio. / Sonatine [a due Violoncelli e] di Liuto e Basso.*

Sonata in A minor

Catalogue No:	Hr 126
Date:	[n.d.]
Key:	A minor
Scoring:	violoncello (2)
Genre:	Violoncello Sonatas

Source description

Original title:	Sonatina a due Violoncelli.
Material:	Manuscript, Autograph, score: 2f.

Incipits

1.1.1 violoncello 1, 3/4 Andante; A minor

1.2.1 3/8 Presto; A minor

Library:	Santini-Sammlung, Diözesanbibliothek, Münster
Siglum/ signature:	D-MÜs/ SANT Hs 3392 (Nr. 9)

Notes:
Title page of Collection: *Originale di Ant. Reggio. / Sonatine [a due Violoncelli e] di Liuto e Basso.*

Sonata in E major

Catalogue No:	Hr 127
Date:	[n.d.]
Key:	E major
Scoring:	violoncello (2)
Genre:	Violoncello Sonatas

Source description

Original title:	Sonatina a due Violoncelli.
Material:	Manuscript, Autograph, score: 2f.

Incipits

1.1.1 violoncello 1, 2/4 Andante; E major

1.2.1 3/8 Presto; E major

Library:	Santini-Sammlung, Diözesanbibliothek, Münster
Siglum/ signature:	D-MÜs/ SANT Hs 3392 (Nr. 10)

Notes:
Title page of Collection: *Originale di Ant. Reggio. / Sonatine [a due Violoncelli e] di Liuto e Basso.*

Sonata in F minor

Catalogue No:	Hr 128
Date:	[n.d.]
Key:	F minor
Scoring:	violoncello (2)
Genre:	Violoncello Sonatas

Source description

Original title:	Sonatina a due Violoncelli.
Material:	Manuscript, Autograph, score: 2f.

Incipits

1.1.1 violoncello 1, 3/4 Andantino; F minor

1.2.1 3/8 Presto; F minor

Library:	Santini-Sammlung, Diözesanbibliothek, Münster
Siglum/ signature:	D-MÜs/ SANT Hs 3392 (Nr. 11)

Notes:
Title page of Collection: *Originale di Ant. Reggio. / Sonatine [a due Violoncelli e] di Liuto e Basso.*

Sonata in C major

Catalogue No:	Hr 129
Date:	[n.d.]
Key:	C major
Scoring:	violoncello (2)
Genre:	Violoncello Sonatas

Source description

Original title:	Sonatina a due Violoncelli.
Material:	Manuscript, Autograph, score: 2f.

Incipits

1.1.1 violoncello 1, c Andante con moto; C major

1.2.1 3/8 Minué.; C major

Library:	Santini-Sammlung, Diözesanbibliothek, Münster
Siglum/ signature:	D-MÜs/ SANT Hs 3392 (Nr. 12)

Notes:
Title page of Collection: *Originale di Ant. Reggio. / Sonatine [a due Violoncelli e] di Liuto e Basso.*

IV Lute Sonatas

1. Index by Key

1. Index by Key:

C Major	Hr 130 Hr 151
C minor	Hr 141
C#minor	Hr 149
D Major	Hr 132 Hr 152
D minor	Hr 137 Hr 153
E Major	Hr 140
E♭Major	Hr 138
E Minor	Hr 145
F Major	Hr 146
F minor	Hr 131
F#minor	Hr 133
G Major	Hr 144
G minor	Hr 135
A♭ Major	Hr 142
A Major	Hr 136
A minor	Hr 134 Hr 150
B Major	Hr 148
B minor	Hr 143
B♭ Major	Hr 134
B♭ minor	Hr 147

Sonata in C major

Catalogue no:	Hr 130
Key:	C major
Scoring:	lute, bass
Genre:	Lute Sonatas

Source description

Original title:	I.
Material:	Manuscript, Autograph, score: 2f.

Incipits

1.1.1 lute, 3/4 Andantino; C major

1.2.1 3/4 Minué.; C major

Library:	Santini-Sammlung, Diözesanbibliothek, Münster
Siglum/ signature:	D-MÜs/ SANT Hs 3392 (Nr. 13)

Notes:
Title page of Collection: *Originale di Ant. Reggio. / Sonatine [a due Violoncelli e] di Liuto e Basso.*

Sonata in F minor

Catalogue no:	Hr 131
Key:	F minor
Scoring:	lute, bass
Genre:	Lute Sonatas

Source description

Original title:	II.
Material:	Manuscript, Autograph, score: 2f.

Incipits

1.1.1 lute, 6/8 Andantino; F minor

1.2.1 3/4 Minué.; F minor

Library:	Santini-Sammlung, Diözesanbibliothek, Münster
Siglum/ signature:	D-MÜs/ SANT Hs 3392 (Nr. 14)

Notes:
Title page of Collection: *Originale di Ant. Reggio. / Sonatine [a due Violoncelli e] di Liuto e Basso.*

Sonata in D major

Catalogue no:	Hr 132
Key:	D major
Scoring:	lute, bass
Genre:	Lute Sonatas

Source description

Original title:	III.
Material:	Manuscript, Autograph, score: 2f.

Incipits

1.1.1 lute, 2/4 Allegretto; D major

1.2.1 3/4 Minué.; C major

Library:	Santini-Sammlung, Diözesanbibliothek, Münster
Siglum/ signature:	D-MÜs/ SANT Hs 3392 (Nr. 15)

Notes:
Title page of Collection: *Originale di Ant. Reggio. / Sonatine [a due Violoncelli e] di Liuto e Basso.*

Sonata in F# minor

Catalogue no:	Hr 133
Key:	F# minor
Scoring :	lute, bass
Genre:	Lute Sonatas

Source description

Original title:	IV.
Material:	Manuscript, Autograph, score: 2f.

Incipits

1.1.1 lute, c Allegretto; F# minor

1.2.1 3/4 Minué.; F# minor

Library:	Santini-Sammlung, Diözesanbibliothek, Münster
Siglum/ signature:	D-MÜs/ SANT Hs 3392 (Nr. 16)

Notes:
Title page of Collection: *Originale di Ant. Reggio. / Sonatine [a due Violoncelli e] di Liuto e Basso.*

Sonata in B♭ major

Catalogue no:	Hr 134
Key:	B♭ major
Scoring:	lute, bass
Genre:	Lute Sonatas
Source description	
Original title:	V.
Material:	Manuscript, Autograph, score: 2f.

Incipits

1.1.1 lute, c Allegro; B♭ major

1.2.1 3/4 Minué.; B♭ major

Library:	Santini-Sammlung, Diözesanbibliothek, Münster
Siglum/ signature:	D-MÜs/ SANT Hs 3392 (Nr. 17)

Notes:
Title page of Collection: *Originale di Ant. Reggio. / Sonatine [a due Violoncelli e] di Liuto e Basso.*

Sonata in G minor

Catalogue no:	Hr 135
Key:	G minor
Scoring:	lute, bass
Genre:	Lute Sonatas

Source description

Original title:	VI.
Material:	Manuscrtipt, Autograph, score: 2f.

Incipits

1.1.1 lute, 3/4 Andante; G minor

1.2.1 3/4 Minué.; G minor

Library:	Santini-Sammlung, Diözesanbibliothek, Münster
Siglum/ signature:	D-MÜs/ SANT Hs 3392 (Nr. 18)

Notes:
Title page of Collection: *Originale di Ant. Reggio. / Sonatine [a due Violoncelli e] di Liuto e Basso.*

Sonata in A major

Catalogue no: Hr 136
Key: A major
Scoring: lute, bass
Genre: Lute Sonatas
Source description
Original title: VII.
Material: Manuscript, Autograph, score: 2f.
Incipits
1.1.1 lute, c Allegro; A major

1.2.1 3/4 Minué.; A major

Library: Santini-Sammlung, Diözesanbibliothek, Münster

Siglum/ signature: D-MÜs/ SANT Hs 3392 (Nr. 19)

Notes:
Title page of Collection: *Originale di Ant. Reggio. / Sonatine [a due Violoncelli e] di Liuto e Basso.*

Sonata in D minor

Catalogue no:	Hr 137
Key:	D minor
Scoring:	lute, bass
Genre:	Lute Sonatas

Source description

Original title:	VIII.
Material:	Manuscript, Autograph, score: 2f.

Incipits

1.1.1 lute, c Allegro; D minor

1.2.1 3/4 Minué.; D minor

Library:	Santini-Sammlung, Diözesanbibliothek, Münster
Siglum/ signature:	D-MÜs/ SANT Hs 3392 (Nr. 20)

Notes:
Title page of Collection: *Originale di Ant. Reggio. / Sonatine [a due Violoncelli e] di Liuto e Basso.*

Sonata in E♭ major

Catalogue no: Hr 138

Key: E♭ major

Scoring: lute, bass

Genre: Lute Sonatas

Source description

Original title: IX.

Material: Manuscript, Autgraph, score: 2f.

Incipits

1.1.1 lute, c Allegro; E♭ major

1.2.1 3/4 Minué.; E♭major

Library: Santini-Sammlung, Diözesanbibliothek, Münster

Siglum/ signature: D-MÜs/ SANT Hs 3392 (Nr. 21)

Notes:
Title page of Collection: *Originale di Ant. Reggio. / Sonatine [a due Violoncelli e] di Liuto e Basso.*

Sonata in A minor

Catalogue no:	Hr 139
Key:	A minor
Scoring:	lute, bass
Genre:	Lute Sonatas

Source description

Original title:	X.
Material:	Manuscript, Autograph, score: 2f.

Incipits

1.1.1 lute, 3/4 Andantino; A minor

1.2.1 3/4 Minué.; A minor

Library:	Santini-Sammlung, Diözesanbibliothek, Münster
Siglum/ signature:	D-MÜs/ SANT Hs 3392 (Nr. 22)

Notes:
Title page of Collection: *Originale di Ant. Reggio. / Sonatine [a due Violoncelli e] di Liuto e Basso*

Sonata in E major

Catalogue no:	Hr 140
Key:	E major
Scoring:	lute, bass
Genre:	Lute Sonatas

Source description

Original title:	XI.
Material:	Manuscript, Autograph, score: 2f.

Incipits

1.1.1 lute, 2/4 Allegro; E major

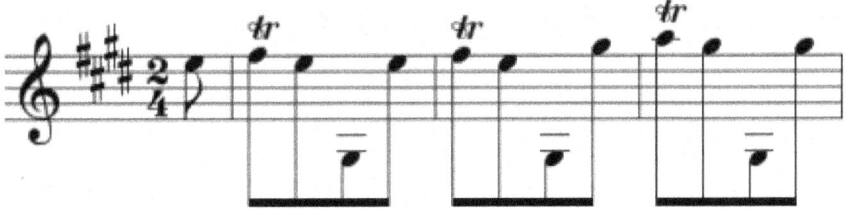

1.2.1 3/4 Minué.; E major

Library:	Santini-Sammlung, Diözesanbibliothek, Münster
Siglum/ signature:	D-MÜs/ SANT Hs 3392 (Nr. 23)

Notes:
Title page of Collection: *Originale di Ant. Reggio. / Sonatine [a due Violoncelli e] di Liuto e Basso.*

Sonata in C minor

Catalogue no:	Hr 141
Key:	C minor
Scoring:	lute, bass
Genre:	Lute Sonatas

Source description

Original title:	XII.
Material:	Manuscript, Autograph, score: 2f.

Incipits

1.1.1 lute, 3/4 Andantino; C minor

1.2.1 3/4 Minué.; C minor

Library:	Santini-Sammlung, Diözesanbibliothek, Münster
Siglum/ signature:	D-MÜs/ SANT Hs 3392 (Nr. 24)

Notes:
Title page of Collection: *Originale di Ant. Reggio. / Sonatine [a due Violoncelli e] di Liuto e Basso.*

Sonata in A♭ major

Catalogue no:	Hr 142
Key:	A♭ major
Scoring Note:	lute, bass
Genre:	Lute Sonatas
Source description	
Original title:	XIII.
Material:	Manuscript, Autograph, score: 2f.

Incipits

1.1.1 lute, c/ Andantino; A♭ major

1.2.1 3/4 Minué.; A♭ major

Library:	Santini-Sammlung, Diözesanbibliothek, Münster
Siglum/ signature:	D-MÜs/ SANT Hs 3392 (Nr. 25)

Notes:
Title page of Collection: *Originale di Ant. Reggio. / Sonatine [a due Violoncelli e] di Liuto e Basso.*

Sonata in B minor

Catalogue no: Hr 143
Key: B minor
Scoring Note: lute, bass
Genre: Lute Sonatas
Source description
Original title: XIV.
Material: Manuscript, Autograph, score: 2f.
Incipits
1.1.1 lute, c Allegretto; B minor

1.2.1 3/4 Minué.; B major

Library: Santini-Sammlung, Diözesanbibliothek, Münster

Siglum/ signature: D-MÜs/ SANT Hs 3392 (Nr. 26)

Notes:
Title page of Collection: *Originale di Ant. Reggio. / Sonatine [a due Violoncelli e] di Liuto e Basso*

Sonata in G major

Catalogue no:	Hr 144
Key:	G major
Scoring:	lute, bass
Genre:	Lute Sonatas

Source description

Original title:	XV.
Material:	Manuscript, Autograph, score: 2f.

Incipits

1.1.1 lute, 3/4 Andantino; G major

1.2.1 3/4 Minué.; G major

Library:	Santini-Sammlung, Diözesanbibliothek, Münster
Siglum/ signature:	D-MÜs/ SANT Hs 3392 (Nr. 27)

Notes:
Title page of Collection: *Originale di Ant. Reggio. / Sonatine [a due Violoncelli e] di Liuto e Basso.*

Sonata in E minor

Catalogue no:	Hr 145
Key:	E minor
Scoring:	lute, bass
Genre:	Lute Sonatas

Source description

Original title:	XVI.
Material:	Manuscript, Autograph, score: 2f.

Incipits

1.1.1 lute, 6/8 Larghetto; E minor

1.2.1 3/4 Minué.; E minor

Library:	Santini-Sammlung, Diözesanbibliothek, Münster
Siglum/ signature:	D-MÜs/ SANT Hs 3392 (Nr. 28)

Notes:
Title page of Collection: *Originale di Ant. Reggio. / Sonatine [a due Violoncelli e] di Liuto e Basso.*

Sonata in F major

Catalogue no:	Hr 146
Key:	F major
Scoring:	lute, bass
Genre:	Lute Sonatas

Source description

Original title:	XVII.
Material:	Manuscript, Autograph, score: 2f.

Incipits

1.1.1 lute, c/ Andantino; F major

1.2.1 3/4 Minué.; F major

Library:	Santini-Sammlung, Diözesanbibliothek, Münster
Siglum/ signature:	D-MÜs/ SANT Hs 3392 (Nr. 29)

Notes:
Title page of Collection: *Originale di Ant. Reggio. / Sonatine [a due Violoncelli e] di Liuto e Basso.*

Sonata in B♭ minor

Catalogue no:	Hr 147
Key:	B♭ minor
Scoring:	lute, bass
Genre:	Lute Sonatas

Source description

Original title:	XVIII.
Material:	Manuscript, Autograph, score: 2f.

Incipits

1.1.1 lute, c Allegretto; B♭ minor

1.2.1 3/4 Minué.; B♭ minor

Library:	Santini-Sammlung, Diözesanbibliothek, Münster
Siglum/ signature:	D-MÜs/ SANT Hs 3392 (Nr. 30)

Notes:
Title page of Collection: *Originale di Ant. Reggio. / Sonatine [a due Violoncelli e] di Liuto e Basso.*

Sonata in B major

Catalogue no: Hr 148
Key: B major
Scoring: lute, bass
Genre: Lute Sonatas
Source description
Original title: XIX.
Material: Manuscript, Autograph, score: 2f.
Incipits

1.1.1 lute, 3/4 Andantino; B major

1.2.1 3/4 Minué.; B major

Library: Santini-Sammlung, Diözesanbibliothek, Münster

Siglum/ signature: D-MÜs/ SANT Hs 3392 (Nr. 31)

Notes:
Title page of Collection: *Originale di Ant. Reggio. / Sonatine [a due Violoncelli e] di Liuto e Basso.*

Sonata in C# minor

Catalogue no:	Hr 149
Key:	C# minor
Scoring:	lute, bass
Genre:	Lute Sonatas

Source description

Original title:	XX.
Material:	Manuscript, Autograph, score: 2f.

Incipits

1.1.1 lute, c Andante; C# minor

1.2.1 3/4 Minué.; C# minor

Library:	Santini-Sammlung, Diözesanbibliothek, Münster
Siglum/ signature:	D-MÜs/ SANT Hs 3392 (Nr. 32)

Notes:
Title page of Collection: *Originale di Ant. Reggio. / Sonatine [a due Violoncelli e] di Liuto e Basso.*

Sonata in A minor

Catalogue no:	Hr 150
Key:	A minor
Scoring:	lute, bass
Genre:	Lute Sonatas

Source description

Original title:	XXI.
Material:	Manuscript, Autograph, score: 2f.

Incipits

1.1.1 lute, 6/8 Larghetto; A minor

1.2.1 3/4 Minué.; A minor

Library:	Santini-Sammlung, Diözesanbibliothek, Münster
Siglum/ signature:	D-MÜs/ SANT Hs 3392 (Nr. 33)

Notes:
Title page of Collection: *Originale di Ant. Reggio. / Sonatine [a due Violoncelli e] di Liuto e Basso.*

Sonata in C major

Catalogue no:	Hr 151
Key:	C major
Scoring:	lute, bass
Genre:	Lute Sonatas

Source description

Original title:	XXII.
Material:	Manuscript, Autograph, score: 2f.

Incipits

1.1.1 lute, 3/4 Andante; C major

1.2.1 3/4 Minué.; C major

Library:	Santini-Sammlung, Diözesanbibliothek, Münster
Siglum/ signature:	D-MÜs/ SANT Hs 3392 (Nr. 34)

Notes:
Title page of Collection: *Originale di Ant. Reggio. / Sonatine [a due Violoncelli e] di Liuto e Basso.*

Sonata in D major

Catalogue no:	Hr 152
Key:	D major
Scoring :	lute, bass
Genre:	Lute Sonatas

Source description

Original title:	XXIII.
Material:	Manuscript, Autograph, score: 2f.

Incipits

1.1.1 lute, 6/8 Andantino; D major

1.2.1 3/4 Minué.; D major

Library:	Santini-Sammlung, Diözesanbibliothek, Münster
Siglum/ signature:	D-MÜs/ SANT Hs 3392 (Nr. 35)

Notes:
Title page of Collection: *Originale di Ant. Reggio. / Sonatine [a due Violoncelli e] di Liuto e Basso.*

Sonata in D minor

Catalogue no:	Hr 153
Key:	D minor
Scoring:	lute, bass
Genre:	Lute Sonatas

Source description

Original title:	XXIV.
Material:	Manuscript, Autograph, score: 2f.

Incipits

1.1.1 lute, c Allegretto; D minor

1.2.1 3/4 Minué.; D minor

Library:	Santini-Sammlung, Diözesanbibliothek, Münster
Siglum/ signature:	D-MÜs/ SANT Hs 3392 (Nr. 36)

Notes:
Title page of Collection: *Originale di Ant. Reggio. / Sonatine [a due Violoncelli e] di Liuto e Basso.*

www.ingramcontent.com/pod-product-compliance
Lightning Source LLC
Chambersburg PA
CBHW020758160426
43192CB00006B/370